D1318036

Environmental Science Experiments

FACTS ON FILE SCIENCE EXPERIMENTS

Environmental Science Experiments

Pamela Walker
Elaine Wood

Facts On File
An imprint of Infobase Publishing

Environmental Science Experiments

Text and artwork copyright © 2010 by Infobase Publishing

Editor: Frank K. Darmstadt
Copy Editor for A Good Thing, Inc.: Betsy Feist
Project Coordination: Aaron Richman
Art Director: Howard Petlack
Production: Victoria Kessler
Illustrations: Hadel Studios

Facts On File, Inc.
An imprint of Infobase Publishing
132 West 31st Street
New York NY 10001

Library of Congress Cataloging-in-Publication Data
Walker, Pam, 1958-
Environmental science experiments / Pamela Walker, Elaine Wood.
p. cm.—(Facts on File science experiments)
Includes bibliographical references and index.
ISBN 978-0-8160-7805-9
1, Environmental sciences–Experiments–Juvenile literature. 2. Science projects–Juvenile literature. I. Wood, Elaine, 1950– . Title.
GE77.W35 2010
507.8–dc22.   2008053715

Facts On File books are available at special discounts when purchased in bulk quantities for businesses, associations, institutions, or sales promotions. Please call our Special Sales Department in New York at 212/967-8800 or 800/322-8755.

You can find Facts On File on the World Wide Web at http://www.factsonfile.com

Text design and composition by A Good Thing, Inc.
Cover printed by Bang Printing, Brainerd, MN
Book printed and bound by Bang Printing, Brainerd, MN
Date printed: August, 2010
Printed in the United States of America

10 9 8 7 6 5 4 3

This book is printed on acid-free paper.

Contents

Preface

For centuries, humans have studied and explored the natural world around them. The ever-growing body of knowledge resulting from these efforts is science. Information gained through science is passed from one generation to the next through an array of educational programs. One of the primary goals of every science education program is to help young people develop critical-thinking and problem-solving skills that they can use throughout their lives.

Science education is unique in academics in that it not only conveys facts and skills; it also cultivates curiosity and creativity. For this reason, science is an active process that cannot be fully conveyed by passive teaching techniques. The question for educators has always been, "What is the best way to teach science?" There is no simple answer to this question, but studies in education provide useful insights.

Research indicates that students need to be actively involved in science, learning it through experience. Science students are encouraged to go far beyond the textbook and to ask questions, consider novel ideas, form their own predictions, develop experiments or procedures, collect information, record results, analyze findings, and use a variety of resources to expand knowledge. In other words, students cannot just hear science; they must also do science.

"Doing" science means performing experiments. In the science curriculum, experiments play a number of educational roles. In some cases, hands-on activities serve as hooks to engage students and introduce new topics. For example, a discrepant event used as an introductory experiment encourages questions and inspires students to seek the answers behind their findings. Classroom investigations can also help expand information that was previously introduced or cement new knowledge. According to neuroscience, experiments and other types of hands-on learning help transfer new learning from short-term into long-term memory.

Facts On File Science Experiments is a six-volume set of experiments that helps engage students and enable them to "do" science. The high-interest experiments in these books put students' minds into gear and give them opportunities to become involved, to think independently, and to build on their own base of science knowledge.

As a resource, Facts On File Science Experiments provides teachers with new and innovative classroom investigations that are presented in a clear, easy-to-understand style. The areas of study in the six-volume set include forensic science, environmental science, computer research, physical science, weather and climate, and space and astronomy. Experiments are supported by colorful figures and line illustrations that help hold students' attention and explain information. All of the experiments in these books use multiple science process skills such as observing, measuring, classifying, analyzing, and predicting. In addition, some of the experiments require students to practice inquiry science by setting up and carrying out their own open-ended experiments.

Each volume of the set contains 20 new experiments as well as extensive safety guidelines, glossary, correlation to the National Science Education Standards, scope and sequence, and an annotated list of Internet resources. An introduction that presents background information begins each investigation to provide an overview of the topic. Every experiment also includes relevant specific safety tips along with materials list, procedure, analysis questions, explanation of the experiment, connections to real life, and an annotated further reading section for extended research.

Pam Walker and Elaine Wood, the authors of Facts On File Science Experiments, are sensitive to the needs of both science teachers and students. The writing team has more than 40 years of combined science teaching experience. Both are actively involved in planning and improving science curricula in their home state, Georgia, where Pam was the 2007 Teacher of the Year. Walker and Wood are master teachers who hold specialist degrees in science and science education. They are the authors of dozens of books for middle and high school science teachers and students.

Facts On File Science Experiments, by Walker and Wood, facilitates science instruction by making it easy for teachers to incorporate experimentation. During experiments, students reap benefits that are not available in other types of instruction. One of these benefits is the opportunity to take advantage of the learning provided by social interactions. Experiments are usually carried out in small groups, enabling students to brainstorm and learn from each other. The validity of group work as an effective learning tool is supported by research in neuroscience, which shows that the brain is a social organ and that communication and collaboration are activities that naturally enhance learning.

Experimentation addresses many different types of learning, including lateral thinking, multiple intelligences, and constructivism. In lateral thinking, students solve problems using nontraditional methods. Long-established, rigid procedures for problem-solving are replaced by original ideas from students. When encouraged to think laterally, students are more likely to come up with unique ideas that are not usually found in the traditional classroom. This type of thinking requires students to construct meaning from an activity and to think like scientists.

Another benefit of experimentation is that it accommodates students' multiple intelligences. According to the theory of multiple intelligences, students possess many different aptitudes, but in varying degrees. Some of these forms of intelligence include linguistic, musical, logical-mathematical, spatial, kinesthetic, intrapersonal, and interpersonal. Learning is more likely to be acquired and retained when more than one sense is involved. During an experiment, students of all intellectual types find roles in which they can excel.

Students in the science classroom become involved in active learning, constructing new ideas based on their current knowledge and their experimental findings. The constructivist theory of learning encourages students to discover principles for and by themselves. Through problem solving and independent thinking, students build on what they know, moving forward in a manner that makes learning real and lasting.

Active, experimental learning makes connections between newly acquired information and the real world, a world that includes jobs. In the 21st century, employers expect their employees to identify and solve problems for themselves. Therefore, today's students, workers of the near future, will be required to use higher-level thinking skills. Experience with science experiments provides potential workers with the ability and confidence to be problem solvers.

The goal of Walker and Wood in Facts On File Science Experiments is to provide experiments that hook and hold the interest of students, teach basic concepts of science, and help students develop their critical-thinking skills. When fully immersed in an experiment, students can experience those "Aha!" moments, the special times when new information merges with what is already known and understanding breaks through. On these occasions, real and lasting learning takes place. The authors hope that this set of books helps bring more "Aha" moments into every science class.

Acknowledgments

This book would not exist were it not for our editor, Frank K. Darmstadt, who conceived and directed the project. Frank supervised the material closely, editing and making invaluable comments along the way. Betsy Feist of A Good Thing, Inc., is responsible for transforming our raw material into a polished and grammatically correct manuscript that makes us proud.

Introduction

During the 20th century, the general public was only vaguely aware that environmental problems were developing on a worldwide basis. Public sentiment started to turn early in the 21st century as governments and scientists began spreading the word that issues concerning the environment are not only real, but are also threatening the sustainability of Earth. Today, very few citizens of this planet are unacquainted with the dangers that challenge the quality of our air, water, and soil. With knowledge comes the responsibility of tackling the predicaments caused by our ever-growing human population.

In *Environmental Science Experiments*, we offer students and teachers some tools to help explore environmental issues. Through 20 new hands-on activities, students can learn more about environmental problems and what can be done to solve them. This volume is part of the new Facts On File Science Experiments set.

For students to become personally involved in issues facing the natural world, they must recognize and understand the problems. Facts, figures, charts, and reports efficiently dispense information about the environment and help raise awareness. However, these delivery systems can make the problems seem too immense for an individual to make a difference. Thankfully, teens and preteens are in a stage of life when they embrace idealistic goals and get involved in causes they feel are important. During middle and high school, teachers can help students see that the actions of each person matter. Science teachers have an opportunity to empower students and put them on the road to making positive changes.

The experiments in this volume examine a variety of environmental problems. Most of the challenges the environment faces are due to the fact that the human population is straining Earth's resources. In the experiment "Population Growth in Yeast," the size and growth patterns of populations are examined to help students understand how the Earth's human population has reached an all-time high in such a relatively short period of time. This experiment also helps students realize the role of education in slowing the rate of population growth.

Environmentalists point out that many problems could be reduced and managed if people would set sustainability as a way of life. A sustainable lifestyle is one that protects resources so that they will be available for future generations. Recycling and source reduction are two ways to help guard resources. Several experiments in this volume address these mainstays of environmental science. In "Do Plants Grow As Well in Gray water As in Tap Water?" students are introduced to gray water and they analyze its usefulness as a recycled item. The experiment "What Do People Throw Away?" takes a close look at the materials that enter the waste stream, the volume of garbage we produce, and the ways in which we dispose of garbage. Two activities, "The Safety of Reusing Water Bottles" and "The Taste Test" get students thinking about why they use plastic bottles and the many ways that plastics impact the environment. In "Design a Reusable Envelope," paper, the main part of the waste stream, is reused and the concept of source reduction expanded.

As the human population grows and lifestyles become more dependent on energy, access to alternative energy is drawing a lot interest. "Solar Energy" and "Wind Energy" are experiments that help students examine the factors involved in using these two energy sources to power our lives. The relatively new field of biofuel is examined in "Algae as Biofuel."

Environmental degradation is also caused by activities carried out by the millions of humans on Earth. Pollution affects all parts of the Earth, including the air, soil, and water. In "Testing Water for Coliform Bacteria," "Effects of Environmental Pollutants on Daphnia," "Build and Use a Turbidity Tube," and "Effects of Nitrates on Duckweed Populations," students examine some of the many problems in our waterways and groundwater. "Biodegradation of Oil" helps students see how scientists can locate and use bacteria to break down oil spilled into water and soil.

In "Density of Invasive Species," students analyze the effects of alien species in ecosystems. Air pollution problems are addressed in "Test for Ozone" and "How Does Acid Precipitation Affect Coleus?" Other experiments in the volume address some of basic principles of environmental science including ecosystem structure and energy transfer.

How can educators help students see themselves as part of the solution to Earth's ills and encourage them to take on a sustainable lifestyle? Perhaps the first step is to remember that people and nature have an innate connection. For some students, this connection is strong and can be easily nourished. Others need opportunities to learn and do more that bonds them to their natural roots. The goal of *Environmental Science Experiments* is to help develop the ideals in students that lead to good stewardship of the planet.

Safety Precautions

REVIEW BEFORE STARTING ANY EXPERIMENT

Each experiment includes special safety precautions that are relevant to that particular project. These do not include all the basic safety precautions that are necessary whenever you are working on a scientific experiment. For this reason, it is absolutely necessary that you read and remain mindful of the General Safety Precautions that follow. Experimental science can be dangerous and good laboratory procedure always includes following basic safety rules. Things can happen quickly while you are performing an experiment—for example, materials can spill, break, or even catch on fire. There will not be time after the fact to protect yourself. Always prepare for unexpected dangers by following the basic safety guidelines during the entire experiment, whether or not something seems dangerous to you at a given moment.

We have been quite sparing in prescribing safety precautions for the individual experiments. For one reason, we want you to take very seriously the safety precautions that are printed in this book. If you see it written here, you can be sure that it is here because it is absolutely critical.

Read the safety precautions here and at the beginning of each experiment before performing each lab activity. It is difficult to remember a long set of general rules. By rereading these general precautions every time you set up an experiment, you will be reminding yourself that lab safety is critically important. In addition, use your good judgment and pay close attention when performing potentially dangerous procedures. Just because the book does not say "Be careful with hot liquids" or "Don't cut yourself with a knife" does not mean that you can be careless when boiling water or using a knife to punch holes in plastic bottles. Notes in the text are special precautions to which you must pay special attention.

GENERAL SAFETY PRECAUTIONS

Accidents can be caused by carelessness, haste, or insufficient knowledge. By practicing safety procedures and being alert while conducting experiments, you can avoid taking an unnecessary risk. Be sure to check the individual experiments in this book for additional safety regulations and adult supervision requirements. If you will be working in a laboratory, do not work alone. When you are working off site, keep in groups with a minimum of three students per group, and follow school rules and state legal requirements for the number of supervisors required. Ask an adult supervisor with basic training in first aid to carry a small first-aid kit. Make sure everyone knows where this person will be during the experiment.

PREPARING

- Clear all surfaces before beginning experiments.
- Read the entire experiment before you start.
- Know the hazards of the experiments and anticipate dangers.

PROTECTING YOURSELF

- Follow the directions step by step.
- Perform only one experiment at a time.
- Locate exits, fire blanket and extinguisher, master gas and electricity shut-offs, eyewash, and first-aid kit.
- Make sure there is adequate ventilation.
- Do not participate in horseplay.
- Do not wear open-toed shoes.
- Keep floor and workspace neat, clean, and dry.
- Clean up spills immediately.
- If glassware breaks, do not clean it up by yourself; ask for teacher assistance.
- Tie back long hair.
- Never eat, drink, or smoke in the laboratory or workspace.
- Do not eat or drink any substances tested unless expressly permitted to do so by a knowledgeable adult.

USING EQUIPMENT WITH CARE

- Set up apparatus far from the edge of the desk.
- Use knives or other sharp, pointed instruments with care.

- Pull plugs, not cords, when removing electrical plugs.
- Clean glassware before and after use.
- Check glassware for scratches, cracks, and sharp edges.
- Let your teacher know about broken glassware immediately.
- Do not use reflected sunlight to illuminate your microscope.
- Do not touch metal conductors.
- Take care when working with any form of electricity.
- Use alcohol-filled thermometers, not mercury-filled thermometers.

USING CHEMICALS

- Never taste or inhale chemicals.
- Label all bottles and apparatus containing chemicals.
- Read labels carefully.
- Avoid chemical contact with skin and eyes (wear safety glasses or goggles, lab apron, and gloves).
- Do not touch chemical solutions.
- Wash hands before and after using solutions.
- Wipe up spills thoroughly.

HEATING SUBSTANCES

- Wear safety glasses or goggles, apron, and gloves when heating materials.
- Keep your face away from test tubes and beakers.
- When heating substances in a test tube, avoid pointing the top of the test tube toward other people.
- Use test tubes, beakers, and other glassware made of Pyrex™ glass.
- Never leave apparatus unattended.
- Use safety tongs and heat-resistant gloves.
- If your laboratory does not have heatproof workbenches, put your Bunsen burner on a heatproof mat before lighting it.
- Take care when lighting your Bunsen burner; light it with the airhole closed and use a Bunsen burner lighter rather than wooden matches.

- Turn off hot plates, Bunsen burners, and gas when you are done.
- Keep flammable substances away from flames and other sources of heat.
- Have a fire extinguisher on hand.

FINISHING UP

- Thoroughly clean your work area and any glassware used.
- Wash your hands.
- Be careful not to return chemicals or contaminated reagents to the wrong containers.
- Do not dispose of materials in the sink unless instructed to do so.
- Clean up all residues and put in proper containers for disposal.
- Dispose of all chemicals according to all local, state, and federal laws.

BE SAFETY CONSCIOUS AT ALL TIMES!

1. Testing Water for Coliform Bacteria

Topic

Water can be tested for the presence of fecal coliform bacteria.

Introduction

Many cities get their water from freshwater surface sources such as lakes, streams, and rivers. These waters naturally contain many types of bacteria. The normal bacterial flora in freshwater includes photosynthetic species as well as decomposers that live on dead matter. However, pathogenic bacteria can also find their way into the waterways. The primary path of pathogenic species is through the fecal matter of humans or other animals. Feces contain bacteria that live in the intestinal tracts of animals. Most of these bacteria are not disease carrying and play roles in digestion and the recovery of nutrients in their animal hosts. However, animal feces may contain bacteria that are *pathogens*.

Local water authorities routinely test water to see if disease-causing agents may be present. Instead of testing directly for pathogenic bacteria, which is expensive, authorities test for the presence of other bacteria carried in feces. *Fecal coliform bacteria*, a large group of organisms that are members of the family Enterobacteriaceae, can be detected through water sampling. Members of this group of organisms are used as indicators for the presence of feces in water. If coliform bacteria are discovered, the water authority may carry out more tests for specific fecal pathogens. In this experiment, you will collect water samples and test them for the presence of coliform bacteria.

Time Required

30 minutes on part A
30 minutes on part B
30 minutes on part C

Materials

- ⏺ sterile plastic collection bottle with lid or sterile test tube with stopper
- ⏺ sterile pipette
- ⏺ sterile petri dish (large)
- ⏺ small beaker
- ⏺ Coliscan Easygel™ (individual use bottle)
- ⏺ aluminum foil
- ⏺ access to hot water
- ⏺ write-on overhead transparency film
- ⏺ transparency pen
- ⏺ small metric ruler
- ⏺ bottle of bleach solution
- ⏺ science notebook

Safety Note Wear gloves when working with water samples. Please review and follow the safety guidelines at the beginning of this volume.

Procedure: Part A

1. Accompany your instructor to the body of water to be tested.
2. Wearing gloves, hold the open collection bottle near its base. Dip the bottle below the surface of the water, but above the bottom.
3. Move the bottle through the water in a U-shaped pattern then bring it to the surface.
4. Pour out a little water so that there is air in top of the bottle. Put the lid on the bottle.
5. Remove your gloves and wash your hands.

Procedure: Part B

1. Wash your hands with soap and clean your work surface.

2. Half-fill the beaker with hot tap water. Soften the Coliscan Easygel™ by putting the bottle in a beaker of hot water for a few minutes.

3. Remove the cap from the bottle of Coliscan Easygel™ and use the sterile pipette to transfer 2.5 milliliters (ml) of your water sample into the softened bottle of Coliscan Easygel™.

4. Put the cap back on the bottle and gently swirl to mix your water sample with the Coliscan Easygel™.

5. Open one side of the sterile petri dish (see Figure 1). Pour the Coliscan Easygel™ into the dish. Replace the top of the petri dish and gently swirl the dish to distribute the gel evenly. Set aside for one hour (hr) or until the gel becomes firm.

6. After the gel is firm, wrap the petri dish in aluminum foil. Invert the petri dish and set it in a warm place.

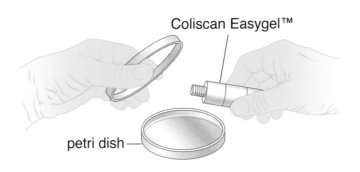

Figure 1

Procedure: Part C

1. After 24 hr (but before 48 hr) unwrap the aluminum foil and examine the petri dish (without removing the top). Look for bacterial colonies, which appear as colored dots.

2. If there are only a few colored colonies, you can easily count them directly. Count and record your findings on Data Table 1 in section A on the row titled "Counts of bacteria." The blue to purple colonies are *Escherichia coli (E. coli)*, one type of coliform bacteria. The magenta to pink colonies are other varieties of coliforms. The colorless colonies are other types of bacteria (see Figure 2).

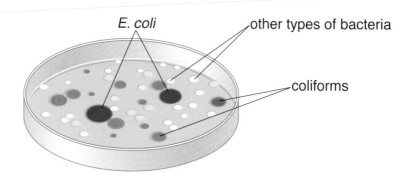

Figure 2

3.   If there are too many colonies to count easily, use the grid method. To do so:

   a. Use a transparency pen to draw a four-box grid on a sheet of transparency film. Make each box in the grid 1 centimeter (cm) (.4 inches [in.]) square (see Figure 3).

   b. Place the grid under the petri dish. (Do not remove the lid from the petri dish).

   c. Count the colored colonies in each box of the grid. Record the counts in section B of the data table in the rows labeled Box 1, Box 2, Box 3, and Box 4. If a colony is growing along the edge of a box, only count it if more than half of the colony is inside the box.

   d. After you have counted the bacteria in each box, move the grid to another position and count again. Chose the position randomly and avoid selecting a section that has a lot of colonies so that you will not skew your results. Record the counts on the data table in the rows labeled Box 5, Box 6, Box 7, and Box 8.

   e. Find the average counts per box, which is also the average number of colonies per centimeter. Write the average on the last row of Data Table 1.

   f. There are about 57.4 square cm (8.9 square in.) in a petri dish, so multiply the average number of colonies by 57.4 to find an estimate of the number of each type of colony in the petri dish.

4.   Since you used 2.5 ml of sample water, multiply the number of colonies (or the average number of colonies) by 40 to find the number of colonies in 100 ml of water.

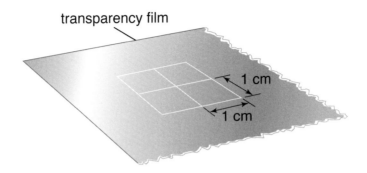

transparency film

1 cm

1 cm

Figure 3

Data Table 1			
	Blue/*E. coli*	**Pink/General coliform**	**No color/Other types bacteria**
A. Easy method			
Counts of bacteria			
B. Grid method			
Box 1			
Box 2			
Box 3			
Box 4			
Box 5			
Box 6			
Box 7			
Box 8			
Average			

5. Following your teacher's directions, pour a small amount of bleach solution in each petri dish and dispose of the dishes.

Analysis

1. What volume of water did you test in this experiment?
2. Why do you think the prepared petri dishes were set aside for 24 hours?
3. From your counts, what was your total (or average) number of colonies of:
    a. *E. coli* per centimeter?
    b. general coliforms per centimeters?
    c. other bacteria per centimeter?
4. What is the purpose of this test?
5. If you tested water from your faucet, what results would you expect? Why?
6. If you tested water from a toilet, what results would you expect? Why?

What's Going On?

Coliform bacteria get their energy by fermenting *lactose*, a sugar. During *fermentation*, the sugar is converted into energy, a gas, and an acid. These bacteria are able to carry out fermentation because they have the *enzymes* necessary to break down sugar. Many coliform bacteria live in water and soil. These "general" coliforms break down sugar with the help of the enzyme galactosidase. One species of coliform, *Escherichia coli* (E. coli) is found in the intestines of animals. *E. coli* produces the enzyme glucuronidase in addition to galactosidase. Coliscan Easygel™ contains two different substrates, each of which reacts with one of the enzymes to produce compounds of different colors

Water authorities check waterways to be sure that total coliform (TC) and fecal coliform (FC) levels fall within safe exposure levels. Total coliform bacteria include those found in the environment, so most are not from the intestinal tracts. In most cases, TC levels are about ten times greater than FC levels. Data Table 2 shows safe levels of coliforms.

Data Table 2
Coliform Standards (colonies per 100 ml of water)

Drinking water	1 TC
Water for swimming	200 FC
Water for boating	1,000 FC

Connections

The primary source of dangerous bacteria in water is human or animal waste. Wastes can enter the water from sources such as pastures, seepage from septic tanks, and overflows or leaks from sewage treatment plants. These pathogens in water can cause serious illness. One of the strains of *E. coli*, 0157:H7, is pathogenic. This is the same strain that has caused illness from eating undercooked ground beef. The first symptoms of infection are severe diarrhea and abdominal cramps about three days after exposure. Complications can include destruction of red blood cells and kidney failure, a condition called *hemolytic uremic syndrome*. Although most people recover, this condition can be fatal.

Want to Know More?

See appendix for Our Findings.

Further Reading

Parrott, Kathleen, Blake Ross, and Janice Woodard. "Microorganisms in Household Water," Virginia Cooperative Extension, April, 2002. Available online. URL: http://www.cdc.gov/nasd/docs/d001201-d001300/d001269/d001269.html. Accessed June 13, 2008. This Web site describes causes, problems, and testing associated with bacterial contamination in water.

Vermont Department of Health. "Coliform Bacteria in Water," 2005. Available online. URL: http://healthvermont.gov/enviro/water/coliform. aspx. Accessed June 13, 2008. This Web site explains why some coliforms can pose a health risk.

Wilkes University. "Water Testing Bacteria, Coliform, Nuisance Bacteria, Viruses, and Pathogens in Drinking Water." Available online. URL: http://www.water-research.net/bacteria.htm. Accessed June 19, 2008. This Web site explains sources of bacteria in drinking water.

2. Effects of Environmental Pollutants on Daphnia

Topic

Daphnia are sensitive to environmental pollutants.

Introduction

Daphnia are small crustaceans that live in both freshwater and seawater. One species of daphnia is shown in Figure 1. Although these tiny animals can be seen with the naked eye, they are best viewed under the *dissecting microscope*. A daphnia's body covering is almost transparent, revealing its internal organs, including the heart, which beats rhythmically. Because daphnia scoot through their watery environments with jerky motions similar to those of jumping fleas, they are known as "water fleas." However, the two types of animals are not closely related.

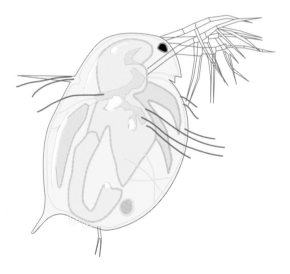

Figure 1

Daphnia

In North America, there are about 150 species of daphnia. Most are herbivores that graze on one-celled algae. Water samples taken from surface water such as ponds, lakes, or streams may yield as many as twenty different species. These tiny animals are an important part of food chain, providing links between photosynthetic organisms and small fish.

Biologists consider daphnia to be indicator organisms, animals whose population size provides information about the condition of the environment. Because daphnia are sensitive to pollution, the presence of some pollutants in relatively low concentrations can drastically reduce their numbers. By counting the number of daphnia in an ecosystem, scientists can keep track of the level of pollution in a waterway. In this experiment, you will expose daphnia to varying amounts of a pollutant to see how they respond.

Time Required

55 minutes on day 1
20 minutes on follow-up days

Materials

- dissecting microscope
- 5 petri dishes
- graduated cylinder
- pipette with 5 millimeter (mm) diameter opening
- daphnia in culture medium
- 200 milliliters (ml) solution (pollutant) to test
- 100 ml distilled water
- wax pen
- stopwatch or clock with a second hand
- science notebook
- 4 small beakers

Safety Note   Please review and follow the safety guidelines at the beginning of this volume.

Procedure: Day 1

1. Transfer one daphnia from the culture medium into a petri dish using a pipette. Place the petri dish on the stage of a dissecting

microscope. Observe the daphnia and notice the following:

a. two long antennae that propel the animal through the water. The antennae are labeled "1" in Figure 2.

b. compound eye, labeled "2."

c. legs that collect food, labeled "3."

d. intestine, where nutrients are absorbed, labeled "4."

e. brood pouch, a place where eggs are incubated, labeled "5."

f. outer shell, labeled "6."

g. heart labeled "7."

h. anus, through which undigested material is eliminated, labeled "8."

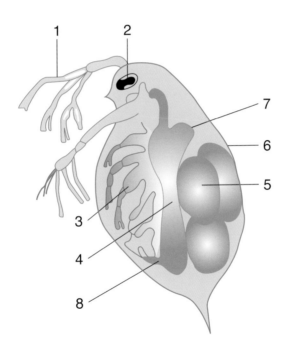

Figure 2

Daphnia anatomy

2. Using the stopwatch, count the number of heartbeats in 1 minute. Record this number in your science notebook.

3. Return this daphnia to the culture medium.

4. Label the petri dishes with a wax pen as: "10," "30," "60," "90," and "control."

5. There are several different solutions available that are potential environmental pollutants. Select one of these solutions to test.

6. Dilute the solution you selected so that you can test its effects on daphnia at various strengths. Use the following recipes to prepare your dilutions in small beakers:

   a. 10 percent: 10 ml of solution and 90 ml of distilled water

   b. 30 percent: 30 ml of solution and 70 ml of distilled water

   c. 60 percent: 60 ml of solution and 40 ml of distilled water

   d. 90 percent: 90 ml of solution and 10 ml of distilled water

7. Pour about 100 ml of distilled water into the "control" petri dish.

8. Pour about 100 ml of each dilution in the appropriate petri dish.

9. Use the pipette to transfer the same number of organisms into each petri dish. Eight to twelve organisms per petri dish will be fine. Try to select young (small) organisms. Record the number of daphnia you place in each petri dish in the column of data table labeled "Start."

10. After one hour (or before the class ends) count the number of surviving daphnia in each petri dish. Remember that daphnia are crustaceans, and they must *molt*, or shed their old shells, to grow. Do not count molted shells as organisms. Molted shells resemble living daphnia, but they are empty.

11. Remove any dead daphnia or molted shells with the pipette.

12. Place the petri dishes in a quiet place until you can check them again at the next class period.

Procedure: Follow-up Days

1. Continue checking the daphnia daily for 2 days more, for a total of 3 days, or until all of them are dead. When you observe the daphnia, record the number of living organisms on the data table. Extend the data table if you want to continue the experiment for more than 3 days. Do not feed the daphnia during the experimental period.

2. Discard any surviving daphnia according to your teacher's instructions.

Analysis

1. What was the heart rate of the daphnia you observed in procedure step 1?

2. What solution did you test during this experiment?

3. How did the strength of the solution you tested affect daphnia survival?

4. What do you think might happen to a pond's food chain if all of the daphnia disappeared? Explain your answer.

5. How do daphnia serve as indicator species in the environment?

	Data Table			
	Number of Living Organisms			
	Start	**After 1 hour**	**Day 2**	**Day 3**
10% solution				
30% solution				
60% solution				
90% solution				
Control				

What's Going On?

Daphnia are very sensitive to changes in their environments. A drop in population size of daphnia suggests that a waterway may contain pollutants. Changes in population sizes can serve as early warnings to scientists that other organisms in the ecosystem may be in danger. Pollutants such as nitrogen and phosphorus-containing compounds may cause an increase in daphnia populations. Nitrogen and phosphorus are two of the nutrients needed for growth of algae. Daphnia feed on algae, so the nutrients could be good in low levels. Higher levels might be problematic.

Connections

Two types of pollution affect organisms in ecosystems: *point source* and *nonpoint source* pollution. Point source pollution comes from one particular place and includes discharges of wastewater into rivers and streams. Point source pollution most often occurs in urban areas. Nonpoint source pollutants are those that wash into waterways from a variety of sources. In rural areas, nonpoint source pollutants are most likely to reach toxic levels in fall or winter when rain is abundant and river flow rates are high.

Some of the chemicals used to protect the environment have unintended negative effects on the organisms. Wildfires can be a serious environmental problem in some areas. One way that firefighters slow wildfires is by spraying them with fire-retardant formulations. Low levels of these fire retardants are generally considered safe for ecosystems, but populations of daphnia and other organisms in the soil of wetlands are drastically reduced when the fall and winter rains wash fire retardants into waterways.

Want to Know More?

See appendix for Our Findings.

Further Reading

Angeler, David, Silvia Martin, and Jose M. Moreno. "Daphnia emergence: a sensitive indicator of fire-retardant stress in temporary wetlands," *Environment International,* Volume 31, Number 4, 2005. Available online. URL: http://cat.inist.fr/?aModele=afficheN&cpsidt=16668515. Accessed June 10, 2008. This research study indicates that even chemicals that are designed to help save the environment, such as fire retardants, can be dangerous to organisms in the ecosystem.

BioMedia Associates. "Swimming, Feeding, and Eating," 2006. Available online. URL: http://ebiomedia.com/gall/classics/Daphnia/daphnia_behave.html. Accessed June 7, 2008. This Web site features a movie of a daphnia showing its heart beating.

Environmental Network News. "Daphnia evolve into pollution eaters," ENN, October 1, 1999. Available online. URL: http://www.cnn.com/NATURE/9910/01/pollution.eaters.enn/index.html. Accessed June 10, 2008. Through natural selection, some species of daphnia have adapted to problems caused by pollutants in their environments.

3. Density of Invasive Species

Topic

Monitoring the density of invasive species is one way to keep track of progress in eradicating plants that damage ecosystems.

Introduction

Invasive species are nonnative organisms that have been moved into ecosystems. Other names for invasive species are exotics, aliens, and nonindigenous organisms. Invasive species can be microbes, fungi, plants, or animals. Although some invasive species cause little damage, others lead to big changes in ecosystems by displacing organisms and changing natural habitats.

To monitor the rate at which an invasive species of plant is spreading through an area, scientists routinely measure the *density*, or the number of plants in a specific area. To find density, scientists could count the plants in an entire study area, but this technique is difficult and time consuming. An easier way is to count the plants in a quadrant, a small region that represents the entire study area. A typical study area measures 100 meters square (m^2). Quadrants within a study area might be 1 m^2. If plants are very dense, smaller quadrants can be used. Likewise, in regions where plants are sparse, larger quadrants are more appropriate.

Thousands of invasive plants have found their way into new ecosystems. Garlic mustard (*Alliaria petiolata*), shown in Figure 1, is a short, herbaceous plant found in most of the United States. This is one of the few plants that can invade and thrive on the floor of deciduous forests. Tree-of-heaven (*Ailanthus altissima*) can be found in every state and thrives in sunny places, even in the cracks of concrete and mortar. In the eastern United States and the Midwest, the vine Japanese honeysuckle (*Lonicera japonica*) is a serious problem. In this experiment, you will determine the density of one or more invasive species of plants that live in your area.

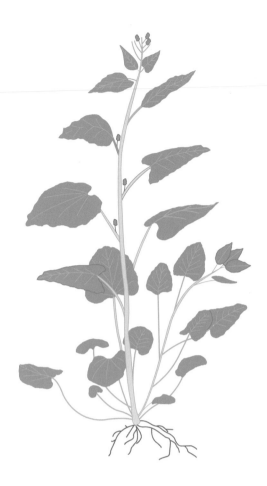

Figure 1

Garlic mustard

Time Required

90 minutes

Materials

- ◦◦ 2 metersticks
- ◦◦ 2 pieces of string that are a little more than 1 meter (m) (39.37 inches [in.]) long
- ◦◦ access to plant identification books
- ◦◦ access to an outdoor area
- ◦◦ science notebook

Safety Note   Please review and follow the safety guidelines at the beginning of this volume.

Procedure

1. Working with a partner, tie one piece of string between the ends of two metersticks. Tie the second piece of string between the other ends of the two metersticks to create a square. You will use this square to measure one quadrant in the study area (see Figure 2).

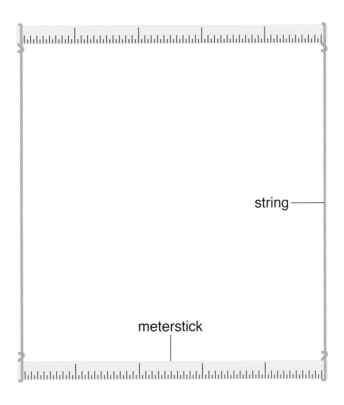

Figure 2

Square used to measure a quadrant

2. Follow your teacher to a predetermined sampling area.

3. To find the quadrant that you will sample, select a random number between 0 and 99. Walk this many steps along the long side of the sampling area. Select another random number between 0 and 99. Walk this many steps into the sampling area. The place where you are standing represents the center of the first quadrant that you will examine. Note the center, then place your square on the ground.

4. Examine the plant species in your quadrant. Write the names of these plants in the first column of the data table. If you do not know the name of a species, collect a stem and take it back to class. Find the name in a plant identification book or from your teacher.

5. Count the number of stems of each species of plant in your quadrant to find the density of each species in quadrant 1. Record your findings on the data table in the column titled "Quadrant 1." Extend the data table as needed.

Data Table			
Names of species	Quadrant 1	Quadrant 2	Quadrant 3

6. Repeat procedure steps 3 through 5 in a second quadrant and label these results as species in quadrant 2.

7. Repeat procedures steps 3 through 5 in a third quadrant and label these results as species in quadrant 3.

8. Determine the density of each species in the entire sampling area. To do so, use the formula:

$$\text{average species density} = \frac{[(\text{density in quadrant 1}) + (\text{density in quadrant 2}) + (\text{density in quadrant 3})]}{\text{total number of quadrants}}$$

Analysis

1. What is an invasive species?

2. Why do you think that invasive species of plants damage ecosystems?

3. Why might a scientist need to know the average density of invasive species in an ecosystem each year?

4. Based on your experimental findings, do you think the average density that you determined for each species in this large plot is fairly accurate? Why or why not?

5. What could you do to get a more accurate average species density?

6. Based on your experimental findings, how did the densities of the invasive species compare to the densities of the native species?

What's Going On?

Invasive species do both economic and ecological damage. Plants that are brought into an ecosystem did not evolve there, so they may not have natural predators or parasites that help keep their numbers in check. As a result, the populations of these plants spread quickly. In a short time, the plants dominate the habitat and replace natural species. Such changes can reduce the *biodiversity* of ecosystems and in some cases lead to the extinction of plants.

Connections

Invasive species of plants are appearing all over the world. Some plants are purposely carried into new habitats and others are transported accidentally during trade. Alligator weed (*Altemanthera philoxeroides*), a South American plant shown in Figure 3, made its way to the United States in the ballast waters of ships. Since its arrival, the plant has reproduced quickly and become a serious problem in southeastern waterways. Alligator weed forms roots easily, then it grows to the surface of the water where it forms a thick, floating mat. Mats prevent drainage of ditches, canals, and other waterways. When mats break lose from their roots, they pile up in the bends of rivers and against bridges, obstructing navigations. Mats also interfere with fishing and swimming and provide breeding grounds for mosquitoes. Alligator weed easily displaces native species along banks. It also blocks needed sunlight from plants that grow in deeper water, causing them to die. Dying mats sink to bottom where they are consumed by oxygen-using bacteria. In a short time, a waterway becomes oxygen depleted. Animals that are mobile leave the area. Slow-moving or immobile animals die.

Figure 3

Alligator weed

Want to Know More?

See appendix for Our Findings.

Further Reading

The Nature Conservancy. "Invasive Species: What You Can Do, Bad Plants in Your Backyard," 2008. Available online. URL: http://www.nature.org/ initiatives/invasivespecies/features/. Accessed June 10, 2008. The extensive Web site shows pictures of many invasive species, explains why they are problems, and details some plans to eradicate them.

The United States National Arboretum. "Invasive Plants," 2007. Available online. URL: http://www.usna.usda.gov/Gardens/invasives.html. Accessed June 13, 2008. This Web site includes pictures of invasive plants, explanations of the problems they cause, and suggestions for getting rid of them.

USDA National Agricultural Library. "Plants." Available online. URL: http://www.invasivespeciesinfo.gov/plants/main.shtml. Accessed June 10, 2008. By clicking on the names of invasive plants, you can access pictures and information.

4. Do Plants Grow As Well in Gray Water As in Tap Water?

Topic
Gray water can be recycled and used to water plants.

Introduction
Water conservation is becoming increasingly important. All the water that is used in the home, except water from toilets and dish washing, is called *gray water*. Toilet and dish water, which can contain dangerous levels of nitrogen and bacteria, is known as *black water*. Gray water includes shower, sink, and laundry water. Although gray water may contain small amounts of hair, oils, particles of food, and other matter, it is not considered to be a health hazard. Gray water and black water usually becomes part of the *sewage*, the wastewater and water-carried solid waste produced by homes and residences. Sewage travels either to the septic tank or to a sewage treatment plant for remediation. At the plant, it is treated to remove solid matter and pollutants and to kill bacteria. Treated sewage is returned to waterways or to the ocean. Some homeowners are reusing their gray water to irrigate plants (see Figure 1). In this experiment, you will design a procedure to compare the growth of plants in gray water and in tap water.

Time Required
55 minutes on day 1
20 minutes on follow-up days

Materials
- tap water (about 1 gallon [g]) (3.8 liters [l]) per group
- gray water (about 1 g [3.8 l] per group)
- 20 seeds (of any type)

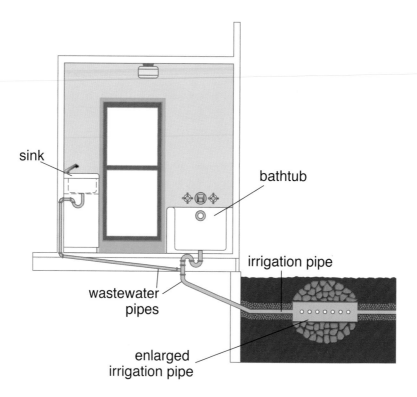

Figure 1

- 20 small pots
- potting soil
- ruler
- triple-beam balance or electronic scale
- science notebook

Safety Note   Wash your hands with antibacterial soap after working with gray water. Please review and follow the safety guidelines at the beginning of this volume.

Procedure

1. Your job is to design and perform an experiment to compare how well plants grow in gray water and in tap water.

2. You can use any of the supplies provided by your teacher, but you will not need to use all of them.

3. Before you conduct your experiment, decide exactly what you are going to do. Write the steps you plan to take (your experimental

procedure) and the materials you plan to use (materials list) on the data table. Show your procedure and materials list to the teacher. If you get teacher approval, proceed with your experiment. If not, modify your work and show it to your teacher again.

4. Keep these points in mind:

   a. Only test one *variable*, not several. In this experiment, the variable is type of water used on the plants. Keep all other factors the same. These include, but are not limited to, temperature, size of containers, and amount of sunlight.

   b. Decide how you want to measure and quantify plant growth. You could measure plant height, plant stem diameter, or plant mass.

5. Once you have teacher approval for your experiment, assemble the materials you need and begin your procedure.

6. Collect your results on a data table of your own design.

Analysis

1. What is gray water?
2. What is the purpose of this experiment?
3. Why must all variables (except the one being tested) be controlled during an experiment?
4. Explain how you controlled the variable of temperature.
5. According to your results, which plants grew better: the ones in tap water or the ones in gray water?

What's Going On?

Gray water is an excellent source of water for indoor and outdoor plants. Plants irrigated with gray water grow as well as those irrigated with water from other sources. Use of gray water has benefits for the environment as well as financial benefits for the community and homeowner. By reusing this water, demand on local water resources such as surface water or underground *aquifers* is reduced. Homeowners do not have to pay for additional water to irrigate shrubbery or lawns. Gray water should not be used on edible plants such as lettuce and carrots, but is ideal for ornamental plants.

Data Table	
Your experimental procedure	
Your materials list	
Teacher's approval	

Gray water can be piped directly onto outdoor plants or it can be diverted through a filtration system made of sand, gravel, and other materials (see Figure 2). In more complex systems, gray water drains into a collection tank, where it is stored for later use. In the storage tank, the water can be cleaned by passing it through a screen and treating it with chlorine to kill any bacteria. Once the gray water is applied to plants, some is used by the plants for metabolic purposes, some evaporates into the air, and the excess percolates through the soil to recharge underground water resource.

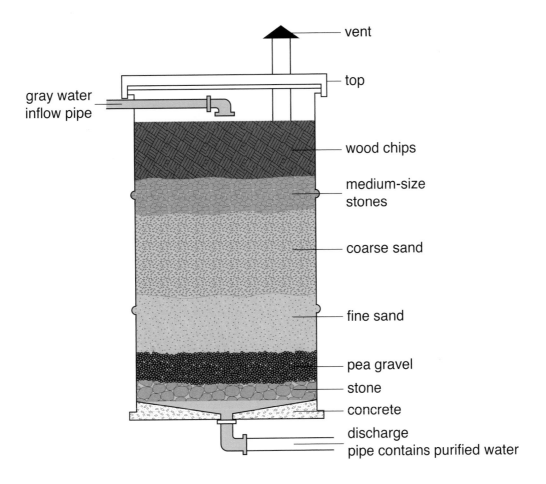

Figure 2

Connections

A family considering a gray water irrigation system can estimate the amount of gray water they will produce by following these steps:

a. Calculate the number of occupants in the home. The first bedroom in the home counts as two occupants and each additional bedroom count as one.

b. Estimate that 40 gallons (gal) (151.42 liters [L]) of gray water will be produced by each occupant.

c. Multiply the number of occupants by the estimated gray water flow per occupant.

The amount of landscape that the family can irrigate with gray water can then be estimated with the following formula:

$$LA = GW$$

where LA equals the landscaped area in square feet and GW equals estimated gray water produced in gallons per week.

Other factors that affect the amount of landscape that can be irrigated include *evapotranspiration*, the amount of water lost through evaporation from soil and plants, the plant types, and the season.

 Want to Know More?

See appendix for Our Findings.

Further Reading

Coder, Kim D. "Using Gray Water on the Landscape," Drought in Georgia. Available online. URL: http://interests.caes.uga.edu/drought/articles/gwlands.htm. Accessed June 13, 2008. Sponsored by the University of Georgia, this Web site explains the advantages and disadvantages of gray water for ornamental plants.

Colorado State University Extension. "Gray Water Reuse and Rainwater Harvesting," March 2008. Available online. URL: http://www.ext.colostate.edu/pubs/natres/06702.html. Accessed June 13, 2008. This Web site explains uses and benefits of gray water.

SAHRA, Arizona Board of Regents. "Residential Water Conservation," 2001. Available online. URL: http://www.sahra.arizona.edu/programs/water_cons/tips/re-use/gray.htm. Accessed June 13, 2008. This Web site defines gray water and discusses its uses.

5. Build and Use a Turbidity Tube

Topic

A turbidity tube can be constructed out of simple materials and used to measure turbidity in local waterways.

Introduction

The clarity of a body of water is one indicator of water quality. Surface waters can become cloudy, or turbid, because of runoff from nearby fields or construction sites, erosion of stream banks, industrial discharge, or excessive growth of unicellular algae. All waterways have normal levels of *turbidity* and the organisms in those water have evolved to live there. But when turbidity levels increase, organisms may not be able to survive.

Turbidity, which can be measured with several different devices, is expressed in Nephelometric Turbidity Units (NTUs). NTUs reflect the amount of light that is scattered by suspended particles in a sample of water. For example, water with a turbidity reading of 10 NTUs is fairly clear and has relatively good visibility, up to 21.5 inches (in.) (54.6 centimeters [cm]). Very turbid water might have a reading of 240 NTUs and a visibility of only 2.5 in. (6.35 cm). Figure 1 shows the visibilities of water at less than 10 NTUs, 200 NTUs, and 1,500 NTUs. Water with high turbidity values can cause stress to inhabitants. Fish reduce their feeding rates and eggs hatch at a slower-than-usual rate. Extended periods of turbidity can lead to fish dying off.

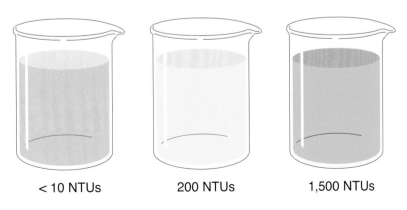

| < 10 NTUs | 200 NTUs | 1,500 NTUs |

Figure 1

Aquatic plants and animals depend on dissolved oxygen (DO) to survive. The concentration of DO in a waterway depends on several factors: temperature, rate of photosynthesis, wave action, amount of oxygen used by bacteria that are breaking down dead organic matter, and turbidity. Turbidity reduces the degree of light penetration, which affects photosynthesis. In addition, suspended particles in turbid water absorb heat from sunlight, causing DO levels to fall. (Warm water holds less oxygen than cool water.) In this experiment, you will make a turbidity tube (see Figure 2) and use it to measure turbidity of water.

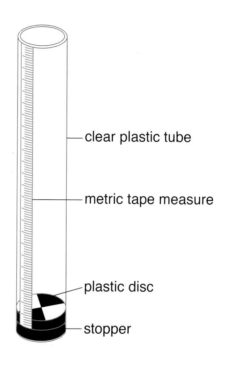

— clear plastic tube

— metric tape measure

— plastic disc

— stopper

Figure 2

Time Required

55 minutes for part A
55 minutes for part B

Materials

- clear plastic tube or fluorescent light sleeve (about 4 feet [ft] [122 centimeters (cm)] long and 1.8 inches [in.][4.5 cm] in diameter)

- 2 rubber bands
- rubber stopper (that will fit into the clear tube)
- white plastic milk jug
- permanent black pen
- scissors
- metric tape measure
- superglue
- collection bottle (about 1.1 quarts [1 liter])
- access to a waterway or a bucket of cloudy water
- science notebook

Safety Note Please review and follow the safety guidelines at the beginning of this volume.

Procedure: Part A

1. Working with a partner, cut out one side of the milk jug so that you have a piece of flat plastic.

2. Stand the clear tube on the piece of plastic. Trace around the clear tube with the black pen.

3. Use scissors to cut the circle of white plastic. Cut around the plastic again to reduce its diameter. Your goal is to create a plastic circle that will fit inside the clear tube.

4. Divide the plastic circle into four equal parts. Color two opposing parts black (see Figure 3).

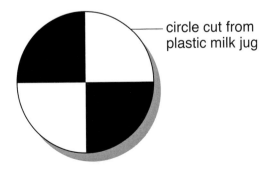

circle cut from plastic milk jug

Figure 3

5. Use superglue to stick the back of the plastic circle to the rubber stopper.

6. Press the rubber stopper into one end of the clear tube.

7. Use two rubber bands to attach the tape measure to the outside of the clear tube. Align the tape measure so that the "0" is even with the black-and-white plastic disc.

8. Put a mark on the clear tube 2.6 in. (6.7 cm) from the black-and-white plastic disk. Label this point at 240 NTU with the permanent black pen.

9. The data table shows the conversion of length to turbidity in NTU. Use the tape measure and the values on the data table to continue marking the tube.

Data Table	
Centimeters	**NTU**
6.7	240
7.3	200
8.9	150
11.5	100
17.9	50
20.4	40
25.5	30
33.1	21
35.6	19
38.2	17
40.7	15
43.4	14
45.8	13
48.3	12
50.9	11
53.4	10
85.4	5

10. Trim the top of the clear tube to just a few centimeters above the last reading.

Procedure: Part B

1. Dip the collection bottle into the waterway. Be careful not to stir the water or to dip up any of the sediment.

2. Stand the turbidity tube upright. Position yourself so that you are between the tube and the Sun, causing a shadow on the tube.

3. Hold your head directly over the tube and look straight down into it (see Figure 4).

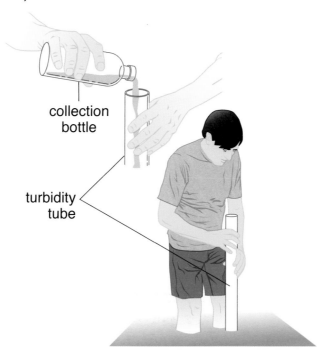

collection bottle

turbidity tube

Figure 4

4. Ask you partner to pour water very carefully from the collection bottle into the turbidity tube, working slowly to avoid creating bubbles. If bubbles begin to form, pause until they disappear.

5. Stop pouring water into the tube as soon as the disk at the bottom of the turbidity tube is no longer visible.

6. Read the value on the side of the turbidity tube and record it in your science notebook.

7. Empty the tube. Repeat steps 1 through 6, swapping jobs with your partner.

8. Record the values found by your classmates.

Analysis

1. What is turbidity?

2. What is the function of the black-and-white disk at the bottom of the turbidity tube?

3. Why do you think the turbidity tube must be completely transparent?

4. Why might a scientist want to measure the turbidity of a stream over time?

5. Did you and your partner get exactly the same values when you read the turbidity of the water sample? Explain why or why not.

What's Going On?

A turbidity tube is a device that shows the correlation between visual cloudiness of water and turbidity. To use the tube, an observer views a marker through a water sample until the marker can no longer be seen. The height of the column of water that obscures the marker is correlated to a turbidity value. Turbidity tubes are excellent and inexpensive tools for field work. Other measurement devices, such as turbidity meters, are also available but are more expensive. Turbidity tubes provide the most accurate data when they are read by three or more individuals. No two individuals have exactly the same vision, so only one person's reading should not be considered sufficient.

Connections

Because many streams and rivers become turbid after a rain, native species of fish are adapted to short-term changes in water. However, in recent years, waterways are remaining turbid for longer periods of time. This difference is due to changes in land use. More soil particles, especially *silts*, are eroding in waterways because of the removal of vegetation along banks. High water turbidity causes problems. Drinking water must have turbidity below 5 NTU. Water turbidity above 10 NTU reduces oxygen levels in waterways and makes it more difficult for organisms to survive. Some types of fish, such as trout, require clear, highly oxygenated water.

To prevent problems due to water turbidity, some communities are limiting the amount of construction that can be done adjacent waterways. By leaving *riparian* regions in their natural states, soil erosion into streams is reduced. Natural riparian ecosystems have other advantages. Regions that border waterways support biologically distinctive communities. In addition, the zones act as natural biofilters that protect waterways from pollution as well as silt.

 Want to Know More?

See appendix for Our Findings.

Further Reading

U.S. Environmental Protection Agency. "Importance of Turbidity," EPA Guidance Manual, April 1999. Available online. URL: http://www.epa.gov/ogwdw/mdbp/pdf/turbidity/chap_07.pdf. Accessed June 13, 2008. This Web page explains the causes and problems due to turbidity.

Water on the Web. "Turbidity," January 17, 2008. Available online. URL: http://waterontheweb.org/under/waterquality/turbidity.html. Accessed June 13, 2008. The natural occurrence of turbidity and changes due to pollutants are discussed.

Waterwatcher. "What Do Waterwatchers Monitor?" February 8, 2006. Available online. URL: http://www.sa.waterwatch.org.au/monitor.htm. Accessed June 13, 2008. This Web site explains several tests done on waterways to monitor water quality and shows how to use a turbidity tube.

6. What Do People Throw Away?

Topic

Analysis of household waste can be used to help plan new and better recycling programs.

Introduction

Whether you call it trash, garbage, or municipal solid waste (MSW), people throw away tons of it each year. Americans dispose of most of their trash in receptacles for removal to solid waste landfills. The function of a landfill is not to get rid of trash; materials in a landfill decompose at an extremely slow rate. Instead, landfills are places where trash is removed from sight. About 80 percent of the trash in this country goes to a landfill like the one in Figure 1. Many landfills are running out of space.

Figure 1

Landfill

A better way to manage resources might be a low-waste tactic. This approach has two major benefits: It reduces waste because materials are reused rather than discarded, and it saves the energy that would have been used to generate new items. Recycling is the keystone behind low-waste management. Currently, only about 13 percent of MSW is recycled. What can be done to improve this statistic?

Before recycling habits can be improved, we first need to know what's in our trash. Analysis of garbage will help establish new and better recycling plans as well as programs to educate people on the importance of recycling. In this experiment, you will analyze the trash produced by several families over a 24-hour period.

Time Required

24 hours for day 1
40 minutes for day 2

Materials

- access to a white board or overhead projector
- calculator (optional)
- science notebook

Safety Note Please review and follow the safety guidelines at the beginning of this volume.

Procedure: Day 1

1. Ask everyone in your household to participate in a survey of the material that goes into the trash over a 24-hour period.

2. Have each person to enter a tally mark on Data Table 1 for each type of trash he or she throws away. Notice that the plastic items in the data table have three categories: PET, HDPE, and Other. *PET* and *HDPE* are recycling codes found on the bottoms of plastic items. Plastic items with any other type of code should be classified as *Other*.

Data Table 1	
Types of waste	**Number of items**
Paper/cardboard/ newspapers	
Plastic, PET	
Plastic, HDPE	
Plastic, other	
Aluminum	
Tin-plated steel cans	
Other metals	
Glass, clear	
Glass, green	
Glass, amber	
Food	
Wood	

Procedures: Day 2

1. Post your family's results with your classmates' on a class data table (like Data Table 1) on the board or overhead projector.

2. Tally the class results. Use your family's data and the class results to help you answer the Analysis questions.

Analysis

1. For your household, calculate:

   a. total plastics

   b. total glass

   c. total metal

2. List the items that your household threw away that are recyclable. (Remember that paper, glass, metal, PET plastic, and HDPE plastic can be recycled.)

3. Examine the class results. Calculate the percentage of the following types of garbage for the entire class:

   a. all types of paper

   b. all types of plastics

   c. all types of glass

   d. all types of metal (includes aluminum, steel cans, and other metals)

   e. all types of food

   f. all types of wood

   To calculate the percentage of each type of garbage, determine the total number of items listed on the data table. Then use the following formula:

   $$\text{percentage of one type garbage} = \frac{\text{no. of one type garbage}}{\text{total no. of items}} \times 100$$

   For example, assume that you, your classmates, and their families threw away a total of 1,000 items and 100 of those items were paper products. To find the percentage of paper items in the trash, your calculations would look like the following:

   $$\text{percentage of paper} = \frac{100}{1,000}$$

   percentage of paper = 0.01 percent

4. Calculate the total number of items on the class data table that are recyclable. Use this number to find the percentage of items that are recyclable.

5. If a person produces 4 pounds (lb.) (1.81 kilograms [kg]) of solid waste each day, how much waste do they produce in 4 weeks? In a year?

What's Going On?

What do people throw away? The national average of the types of materials that people throw away is shown in Figure 2.

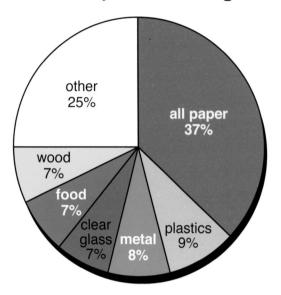

Figure 2
Material thrown away

According to Environmental Protection Agency, U.S. citizens average four pounds of solid waste per person per day.

One of the best ways to reduce the amount of waste we produce is to recycle. Recycling is good for the environment on several levels. When a material is recycled, we save the energy that would have been used to extract the raw materials, transport those raw materials, and produce more of those products. Recycling also reduces greenhouse gases, saves space in landfills, and cuts back on the amount of raw resources that are mined.

Connections

Paper is the primary type of trash in MSW. For every 100 lb (45 kg) of trash, 37 lb (16.7 kg) is paper. Some of the types of paper that are discarded include newsprint, cardboard, and the stuffing in diapers. Paper is made from trees that are cut, transported, chopped into small pieces, and pulped in a chemical process that removes everything but the wood fibers. The product is bleached and coated with finishers like clay and adhesive to produce a glossy finish. All of these processes involve energy and fossil fuels. On the other hand, the manufacture of paper products from recycled materials uses 40 percent less energy than paper made from trees.

Glass is more difficult than paper to recycle because it must be separated by colors. Of the materials recycled, glass makes up less than 10 percent. However, efforts to recycle glass are well worth the trouble. Recycling two glass bottles saves enough energy to boil five cups of water. After discarded glass is separated by color, it is broken into small pieces called *cullet,* which is heated with silica, sand, soda ash, and limestone. The product is molded into new containers, cooled, and shipped to manufacturers (see Figure 3).

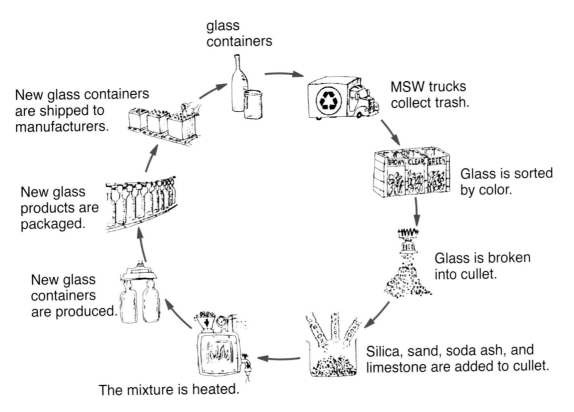

Figure 3

The life of a glass container

Plastics must be recycled according to their types. The two most common types of plastics are polyethylene terephthalate (PET) and high density polyethylene (HDPE). Soft drink bottles, water bottles, and many food containers are made of PET. HDPE is most commonly used to make containers for milk, juice, cosmetics, and cleaners.

Metals are the most commonly recycled items because they bring the greatest cash rewards. Every day, American use 200 million aluminum cans. Like many other natural resources, aluminum does not exist in the pure form. In nature, it is found as an ore called alumina that contains oxygen. To free aluminum from the ore, it must be heated in a smelter then separated with a powerful electric current. These processes require a lot of energy, so recycling aluminum is a big energy savings. Making cans from recycled aluminum uses only 4 percent of the energy of making cans from ore. By recycling one aluminum can, you save as much energy as is contained in one cup of gasoline.

Want to Know More?

See appendix for Our Findings.

Further Reading

How Stuff Works. "How Landfills Work." Available online. URL: http://www.howstuffworks.com/landfill.htm. Accessed June 19, 2008. This Web site provides an easy-to-read explanation of the structure and function of landfills.

National Institute of Environmental Health Sciences. "Reduce, Reuse, and Recycle," January 22, 2008. Available online. URL: http://kids.niehs.nih.gov/recycle.htm. Accessed June 19, 2008. Commonsense suggestions for recycling are provided along with tips for dealing with toxic materials such as batteries and paints.

Waste Online. "Paper Recycling," January 6, 2008. Available online. URL: http://www.wasteonline.org.uk/resources/InformationSheets/paper.htm. Accessed June 19, 2008. This Web site provides details on paper recycling and links to other resources on recycling.

7. Solar Energy

Topic

Solar energy can be measured with a voltmeter and milliammeter.

Introduction

What would your life be like without electricity? Today's society depends on electrical power to keep our homes warm, provide light, power computers, run refrigerators, and heat ovens. Most electricity comes from burning fossil fuels such as coal and oil, two *nonrenewable resources*. The production of electricity from these fossil fuels gives off dangerous air pollutants including carbon dioxide, which is linked to *global warming*, and oxides of sulfur and nitrogen, two components of *acid rain*.

A cleaner, more efficient source of energy is readily available: the Sun. Located about 93 million miles (about 149 million kilometers) away, the Sun is able to meet all of our power needs. In fact, the amount of energy that Earth receives from the Sun each minute could power every home and business for a year. All we need to do is develop an efficient and affordable method of harnessing this energy.

One way to capture energy from the Sun is to convert it into electricity with a *solar cell* (see Figure 1). When light hits compounds within a solar cell, some energy is absorbed, some is reflected, and some passes through. The energy that is absorbed can free electrons in those compounds from their chemical bonds. Freed electrons create vacancies into which other electrons can move. This movement of electrons is electricity. Solar cells produce *direct current* (DC), electrical energy that flows in only one direction, like a current from a battery. The amount of electrical power that solar cells yield depends on the size and number of cells and the brightness of the Sun's light. Electrical power can be calculated with the following formula:

$$P = V \times I$$

where P represents power in watts, V stands for voltage, and I represents the amount of current of amps. In this experiment, you will build an electrical circuit that contains a solar cell, a DC solar motor, a milliammeter, which measures current in milliamps (mA) and a voltmeter, a device that measures voltage.

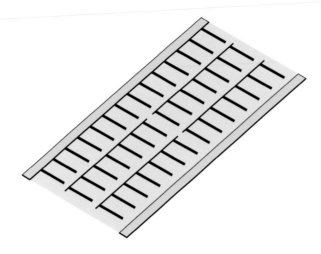

Figure 1

Solar cell

Time Required

55 minutes

Materials

- solar cell (1.5 volt [V] or greater)
- DC solar motor
- milliammeter
- voltmeter
- 6 lead wires with alligator clips on both ends
- small piece of masking tape
- index card
- science notebook

Safety Note   Take care when working with electrical circuits. Please review and follow the safety guidelines at the beginning of this volume.

Procedure

1. Set up the circuit shown in Figure 2.

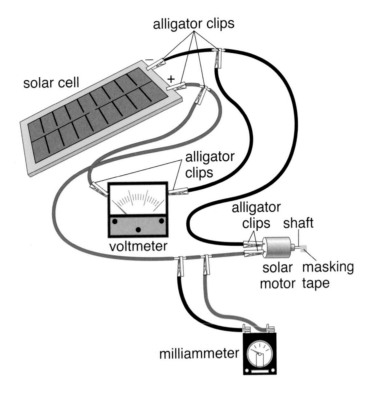

Figure 2

2. Place a small piece of masking tape on the shaft of the DC solar motor so that you can easily observe rotations of the shaft.

3. Expose the solar cell to direct sunlight. Observe the voltmeter and record the voltage passing through the circuit in your science notebook.

4. Observe the milliammeter and record the current (*I*) in milliamps. Convert milliamps to amps and record the result in your science notebook. Remember that 1 amp is the same as 1,000 milliamps.

5. Count the number of times the DC solar motor shaft turns in 15 seconds and record the number in your science notebook.

6. Cover half of the solar cell with an index card.

7. Repeat steps 3 through 5.

Analysis

1. Calculate the power output of the solar cell using the formula:

   $P = V \times I$

   In this calculation, use the voltage and amperage you recorded during the first part of the experiment.
2. Use the same formula to calculate the power output of half the cell.
3. Explain how the number of rotations of the DC solar motor changed when half of the solar cell was covered. What caused this change?
4. How could you create a circuit that would produce more electricity?
5. Suggest some uses for solar cells.
6. What are the benefits of solar energy?
7. Suggest some drawbacks or problems using solar energy.

What's Going On?

In this experiment, the solar cell is the source of electrical power and the part of the circuit that uses electricity is the DC solar motor. The milliammeter measures the current flowing through circuit and the voltmeter measures voltage across the solar cell. These measurements make it possible for you to calculate the power output of the solar cell.

Solar cells produce maximum output when bright sunlight strikes them directly. Maximum solar output extends from 9 A.M. to 3 P.M. Anything that reduces solar energy reduces the output of the circuit. Cloud cover, smog, fog, and other weather conditions as well as shade trees and tall buildings can interfere with the efficiency of solar cells. To increase electrical output, dozens of solar cells are packaged together in glass housings to form solar modules.

Connections

The French scientist Alexandre-Edmond Becquerel (1820–91) made a remarkable discovery in 1839—he found that some materials give off electricity when sunlight strikes them. This *photo* (light) *voltaic* (electric) effect led to the idea of using these materials as generators of electricity. In the 1950s, scientists working in Bell Laboratories used silicon compounds to create solar cells that changed 4 percent of energy striking the device into electricity. Since that time, scientists have been working to make solar cells more efficient and cost effective.

Solar cells produce direct current, so they require a device to change the electricity to *alternating current* (AC). In an AC circuit, electricity reverses its direction of flow about 50 or 60 times each second. Your home and the school are powered with alternating current. Solar cells are currently used to provide power in remote areas where connection to a power grid is not possible. They also run orbiting satellites, emergency telephones, navigational buoys, billboards, and street lights. Scientists hope to develop solar cells that can power homes, cars, and industries.

Want to Know More?

See appendix for Our Findings.

Further Reading

Florida Solar Energy Center. "Does the 'Sunshine' State Have a Sufficient Solar Resource to Support Solar Energy Applications?" March 27, 2007. Available online. URL: http://www.fsec.ucf.edu/en/media/enews/2007/2007-04_Sunshine_state.htm. Accessed June 15, 2008. A map of the United States shows the relative amounts of solar energy each state receives.

Hiebert, Ron. "Investing in Solar," *Edmonton Sun*, June 15, 2008. Available online. URL: http://www.edmontonsun.com/Business/News/2008/06/15/5882351-sun.html. Accessed June 15, 2008. Heibert discusses recent advances in solar energy technology.

ScienceDaily. "Solar Energy News" Available online. URL: http://www.sciencedaily.com/news/matter_energy/solar_energy/. Accessed June 15, 2008. This Web site is collection of news articles on solar energy.

8. The Safety of Reusing Water Bottles

Topic

Water bottles that are reused may harbor bacteria.

Introduction

Humans, like all living things, must have water to survive. Water is the medium in which biochemical reactions take place. This compound is so important that it makes up about 60 percent of the human body. Water lost through metabolic processes must be replaced. So how much water should you drink daily? There is no simple answer to this question, but some experts recommend 13 cups (about 3 liters [L]) for men and 9 cups (2.2 L) for women.

One convenient way to have access to water all day is to carry a water bottle. These easy-to-carry containers can be packed in backpacks, briefcases, and purses. Since most people drink more than one bottle of water each day, many folks refill their empty bottles at water fountains and taps. Some people refill bottles to save money and others do so to reduce the amount of plastic entering landfills. Whatever the reason, reuse of water bottles is a common practice. All of this refilling of bottles without washing leads to the question: Is it safe to drink water from a refilled bottle? To find out, you will take swabs from new and used water bottles. Each swab will be spread across a sterile *agar* plate, a gelatinlike material that contains nutrient growth medium to detect bacteria.

 Time Required

20 minutes for Part A
30 minutes for Part B
30 minutes for Part C

Materials

- ☛ 4 petri dishes with prepared agar plates
- ☛ 4 sterile swabs
- ☛ 4 bottles of water (same brand)
- ☛ incubator
- ☛ 3 volunteers
- ☛ rubbing alcohol in a spray bottle
- ☛ small beaker of diluted bleach
- ☛ paper towels
- ☛ antibacterial soap
- ☛ permanent marker
- ☛ bleach solution
- ☛ science notebook

Safety Note Wash your hands with antibacterial soap after working with swabs and petri dishes. Take care when working with bleach solution to keep if off of your skin. Wear gloves and goggles or safety glasses. Please review and follow the safety guidelines at the beginning of this volume.

Procedure: Part A

1. Four days before the experiment, find three volunteers (from your school, neighborhood, or home) who are willing to use a water bottle for three days without washing the bottle between refills. Record the names of the volunteers in your science notebook.

2. Write each volunteer's name on a water bottle. Tell each volunteer to:
   a. drink the water in the bottle.
   b. refill the bottle at least three times a day for the next three days (without washing) and drink the water.
   c. return the bottle to you on the fourth day.

Procedure: Part B

1. Wash a lab table or other work surface with antibacterial soap or cleanser and wipe dry with paper towels.

2. Lightly mist the work surface with alcohol and let dry.

3. Wash and dry your hands, then mist them with alcohol.

4. Place the three water bottles from your volunteers on the work surface. Place a new, unopened bottle of the same type of water on the work surface.

5. Place four petri dishes on the work surface.

6. Open one of the used water bottles and place the cap on the work surface. Open the plastic wrap on a sterile swab. Remove the swab (without touching the cotton tip). Run the cotton tip of the swab around the mouth of the water bottle.

7. Open the lid to one of the petri dishes. Holding the lid in one hand, gently rub the swab across the agar in a zigzag pattern (see Figure 1). Replace the lid.

8. Dip the cotton swab in the diluted bleach solution, then dispose of it according to your teacher's directions.

9. Label the petri dish with the name on the water bottle.

10. Repeat steps 5 through 9 with the other bottles.

11. Turn the petri dishes upside down and incubate at about 100 degrees Fahrenheit (°F) (37 degrees Celsius [°C]) for 24 to 48 hours.

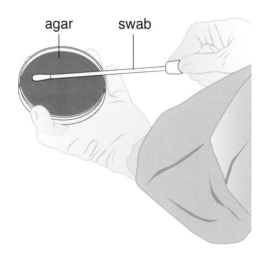

Figure 1

Procedure: Part C

1. Remove the petri dishes from the incubator. Bacterial colonies appear as spots on the agar (see Figure 2). Without opening the petri dish, count the number of colonies on each plate. Record the number in your science notebook.

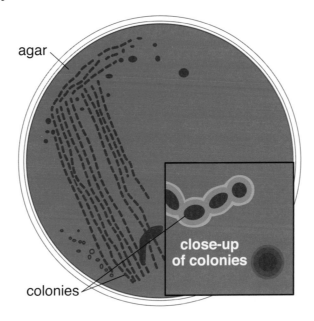

agar

colonies

close-up of colonies

Figure 2

2. When you are finished with an agar plate, destroy the bacterial colonies by pouring a small amount of diluted bleach solution over the agar. Dispose of agar plates according to your teacher's directions.

Analysis

1. Which petri dish(es) showed the most bacterial growth?

2. What conclusions can you draw about the safety of reusing water bottles?

3. Suggest a follow-up experiment that would give you more information about bacterial growth on water bottles.

4. Why do you think bleach is used on the cotton swabs and the petri dishes?

5. Suggest some safe ways to carry water to school.

What's Going On?

An agar plate is a petri dish that contains nutrient agar, a gelatinlike medium that will support the growth of bacteria. Nutrient growth media vary in color, depending on their ingredients, from tan to deep red. One or two days after swabbing, bacteria picked up on the swabs start forming small colonies on the agar plates. Hundreds of types of bacteria will grow on nutrient agar. Most of these bacteria are harmless, but *pathogens,* disease-causing organisms, can grow there also. For this reason, surfaces that contain bacteria must be disinfected with a bleach solution.

In some cases, different types of bacteria growing on agar can be distinguished by visual examination of the colonies. To further differentiate bacterial types, more studies are required. Samples of the bacteria can be transferred to other petri dishes containing different types of specialized media. Not all bacteria will grow on the same specialized media. Bacterial colonies can be further examined under the microscope after staining. One of the most common staining techniques is *gram staining.* Microorganisms that turn blue when stained with crystal violet are classified as gram positive. These microbes include some staphylococci and streptococci. Gram negative bacteria are those that do not take up the gram stain and they include *Escherichia coli* and *Vibrio cholerae.*

Connections

Plastic water bottles are designed for one-time use. Bacteria enter the bottles when the drinker's lips or hands touch the necks. Washing bottles with soap and water removes some, but not all, bacteria. Most of the bacteria growing at the mouth of the bottles are harmless, but pathogens, may be present. In some cases, bottles show high counts of bacteria, including *fecal coliform* bacteria such as *E. coli.* These bacteria are found in the intestines of mammals. Most likely, the bacteria entered the water bottles from the hands and mouths of students.

Should plastic water bottles be reused? The answer to this question is complex, involving health and environmental issues. Public health officials do not recommend washing and reusing bottles. Washing is rarely thorough, so some bacteria persist. Repeated washing can damage the plastic. From the environmental point of view, the bottles themselves are problematic because there are so many of them. Sales of bottled water have quadrupled in the last 20 years. Bottles are made from petroleum, a nonrenewable resource, and more petroleum products are used to ship them to their destinations. One brand of bottled water taken from a spring on an island in the Pacific is shipped worldwide. The processes required to make each one-liter bottle of water produce about one-half pound of greenhouse gases.

 Want to Know More?

See appendix for Our Findings.

Further Reading

Gashler, Krisy. "Thirst for Bottled Water Unleashes Flood of Environmental Concerns," The Ithaca (N.Y.) Journal, *USA Today*, June 7, 2008. Available online. URL: http://www.usatoday.com/news/nation/environment/2008-06-07-bottled-water_N.htm. Accessed June 11, 2008. Gashler examines the environmental impact of bottled water.

KITV. "Refilling Your Water Bottle Turns It Into a Bottle of Bacteria," May 19, 2003. Available online. URL: http://www.kltv.com/global/story.asp?s=8945. Accessed June 10, 2008. In this interesting article, the author discusses water bottles that were used a week by volunteers then cultured for bacteria.

Tugend, Alina. "The (Possible) Perils of Being Thirsty While Being Green," *New York Times,* January 5, 2008. Available online. URL: http://www.nytimes.com/2008/01/05/business/smallbusiness/05shortcuts.html?pagewanted=2&sq=plastic%20water%20bottles&st=cse&scp=1. Accessed July 28, 2008. Tugend examines some of the varying opinions about water bottle contaminates.

9. Wind Energy

Topic

Wind is an alternative energy source that can be used to generate electricity.

Introduction

The Sun is the source of energy for Earth. Sunlight is not evenly distributed, so some areas receive more solar energy than others. In regions that are heated by intense Sun rays, air rises. Areas of cooler air rush in to take the place of the rising, warm air. This moving air is *wind*.

The *kinetic energy* of wind can be used to generate electricity using a windmill. Wind turns the blades of a windmill, which are connected to a shaft. As the shaft rotates, it powers an electrical *generator*, a device that produces electricity by moving a magnet through a coil of wire. Electricity travels to *transformers* that convert the electricity into a form that can travel along transmission lines (see Figure 1). In this experiment, you will design blades for a windmill then test the blades to see how they affect the voltage produced by that windmill.

Time Required

45 minutes

Materials

- ➼ small fan or hair dryer
- ➼ small DC motor (1.5 to 15 volts [V])
- ➼ cork (at least 0.8 inches [in.] [2 centimeters (cm) in diameter])
- ➼ voltmeter (or multimeter)
- ➼ 2 lead wires with alligator clips on both ends
- ➼ 4 paper clips

- index card
- tape
- scissors
- science notebook

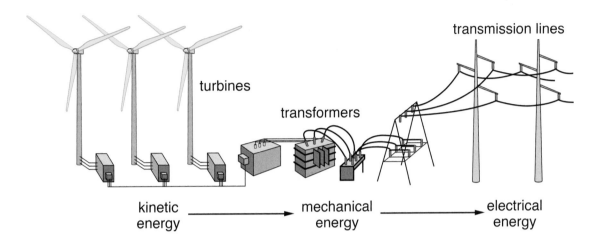

transmission lines

turbines

transformers

kinetic energy → mechanical energy → electrical energy

Figure 1

Safety Note   Take care when working with electrical currents. Please review and follow the safety guidelines at the beginning of this volume.

Procedure

1. Set up the circuit shown in Figure 2.
2. Push the cork onto the shaft of the DC motor so that it turns when the motor is running.
3. Use paper clips, index card, scissors, and tape to construct windmill blades to attach to the cork. Your blades should be able to capture wind (from the fan or hair dryer) to turn the shaft. When your blades are complete, attach them to the cork. You have a simple windmill.
4. Turn on the fan or hair dryer and point it toward the windmill. As the blades turn, observe the voltmeter. Record the voltage passing through the circuit in your science notebook.
5. Change the shape of the windmill blades and repeat step 4.
6. Change the size of the windmill blades and repeat step 4.
7. Change the angle of the windmill blades and repeat step 4.

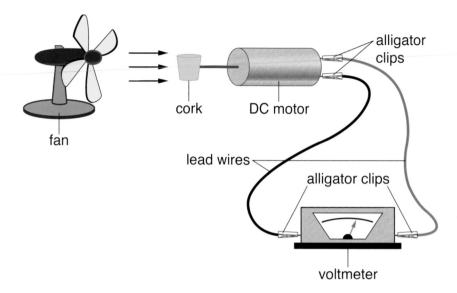

Figure 2

Analysis

1. What is the function of the voltmeter in this experiment?

2. Describe the shape, size, and angle of blades that produced the most electricity.

3. In this experiment, you only produced a very small amount of electricity. Suggest some ways to produce more electricity in the laboratory.

4. What are some advantages of wind-generated electricity? What are some disadvantages?

5. Suggest some uses for wind-generated electricity.

What's Going On?

In this experiment, the moving air from the fan or hair dryer turns the blades of the simple windmill, causing the shaft to turn and generate a small amount of electricity. The basic unit for measuring electrical strength is a *volt*, the force needed to send a certain amount of electrical energy through a circuit. Voltage is measured by the voltmeter. The amount of voltage produced by the spinning windmill blades depends on several factors, including the speed of the blades. The speed of blades depends on the speed of wind and the design and arrangement of the blades. Blade length is an important factor because length is directly proportional to the swept area, the space covered by the blades. The greater the swept area, the more wind caught with each revolution. Blades must be set at an angle that allows them to capture the wind.

Connections

Windmills, also known as wind turbines, are sometimes clustered in large areas called wind farms. In the United States, wind farms supply about 10,000 megawatts (MW) of electricity, enough to power 2.5 million homes, or less than 1 percent of the energy produced. The largest of these farms is Horse Hollow, a 100-acre (40.5-hectare) development in Texas that houses 421 wind turbines. Texas is number one in wind-generated electricity, followed by California, Iowa, Minnesota, and Oklahoma. Most energy-producing plants are owned by public utility companies. Wind farms are different; they are usually run by businesses that sell the electricity they produce to public utilities.

Generation of electricity using the wind offers many advantages over traditional, coal-powered power plants. Wind, a *renewable resource*, is clean and does not produce carbon dioxide, a culprit in *global warming*, or oxides of sulfur and nitrogen, which contribute to *acid rain*. Compared to other electricity-producing technologies, wind power is economical. As a result, development of wind farms reduces the number of fossil fuel plants needed. Despite these pluses, wind farms are not a perfect solution to our growing energy demands. Winds must be blowing at a minimum of 15 miles per hour (mph) (24.14 kilometers per hour [kph]) to produce electricity, so not all locations can support turbines. Wind turbines are tall and obvious, and many people think they are unattractive. In addition, some migrating birds collide with wind turbines. As with all technologies, citizens must weigh the advantages and disadvantages of wind farms.

Further Reading

American Wind Energy Association. Available online. URL: http://www.awea.org/. Accessed June 20, 2008. This Web site offers information on legislation, policies, resources, and educational "web tutorials" pertaining to wind-powered generators.

Energy Kids Page. "Wind Energy—Energy From Moving Air," November 2007. Available online. URL: http://www.wired.com/science/planetearth/news/2005/10/69177. Accessed June 20, 2008. A simple explanation of technology used to harness wind energy is offered on this Web site.

Wade, Will. "Unexpected Downside of Wind Energy," *Science: Planet Earth*, October 14, 2005. Available online. URL: http://www.wired.com/science/planetearth/news/2005/10/69177. Accessed June 20, 2008. Wade reports on the problems that wind farms pose to birds.

10. Test for Ozone

Topic

Levels of ozone in an area can be measured with Schonbein test paper.

Introduction

Oxygen(O_2), is the life-supporting gas we breathe. However, *ozone* (O_3), is a chemically reactive and corrosive gas made of three chemically bonded oxygen atoms. Because of its high reactivity, ozone irritates delicate tissues in the eyes, throat, and lungs. Ozone also damages some synthetic materials like rubber, electrical wire coatings, fabrics, and paint.

Ozone is found in two parts of the atmosphere. In the *stratosphere*, an upper layer, it protects the Earth from damaging ultraviolet radiation. In the *troposphere*, the layer closest to Earth, ozone naturally occurs at low levels. However, at high concentrations, the chemical is a pollutant. High levels of ground-level ozone are produced in a series of complex chemical reactions caused by sunlight and the unburned hydrocarbons. These compounds result from combustion of fossil fuels in vehicles, industries, and power plants. As the size of the human population increases, ground-level ozone is likely to increase with it. In this experiment, you will prepare a test that indicates the presence of ozone then use it to check several locations in your area for ground-level ozone.

Time Required

45 minutes on part A
15 minutes on part B
45 minutes on part C

Materials

- beaker (200 to 300 milliliters [ml])
- 5 grams (g) of cornstarch
- 1 g of potassium iodide

- 100 ml water
- hot plate
- hot mitts
- glass stirring rod
- filter paper (1 sheet)
- small brush
- drying oven or microwave oven (optional)
- scissors
- 6 Ziploc™ bags
- spray bottle of distilled water
- 6 clothespins
- bulb psychrometer or access to local weather information
- science notebook

Safety Note   Wear gloves and goggles or safety glasses when working with potassium iodide. Take care when using the hot plate. Please review and follow the safety guidelines at the beginning of this volume.

Procedure: Part A

1. Place 100 ml of water and 5 g of cornstarch in the beaker. Put the beaker on the hot plate and heat, stirring to mix the contents. Continue heating and stirring until the mixture gels.

2. Wear hot mitts to remove the beaker from the hot plate. Add 1 g potassium iodide and stir well. Let the beaker and its contents cool.

3. Place a piece of filter paper on the table. Use the brush to evenly spread the contents of the beaker on one side of the filter paper. Turn the paper over and coat the other side as well.

4. The paper can be used to test for ozone at this point, or it can be dried and store for later use. To dry, place the paper in a low-temperature drying oven or in a microwave for about 40 seconds. Alternately, use a clothespin to hang the paper out of the Sun's direct rays until it dries.

5. When the paper is dry, cut it into strips that are about 1 inch (in.) (2.5 centimeters [cm.]) wide. Store the strips in a Ziploc™ bag.

Procedure: Part B

1. Take a few strips of ozone-testing paper home with you and use clothespins to secure them in outdoor areas. Make sure that they are not in direct sunlight. Spray the strips with distilled water. Leave the strips for at least 8 hours.

Procedure: Part C

1. The next day, collect the strips, label them with date and location, and place them in the Ziploc™ bags.

2. Spray the papers with distilled water, examine them, and compare their colors to the Schonbein color scale, which translates color to levels of ozone (see Figure 1). Record your findings in your science notebook.

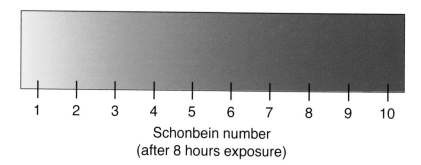

Schonbein number
(after 8 hours exposure)

Figure 1

3. Find the relative humidity in your area in one of two ways. If you have a bulb psychrometer, use it to record relative humidity at each of the locations where you hung a strip. Record the relative humidity from each location in your science notebook. If you do not have a bulb psychrometer, consult your local weather information. Round off the relative humidity to the nearly 10 percent.

4. Relative humidity affects the accuracy of the ozone test paper. High humidity makes the paper more sensitive to ozone. To accommodate this, relative humidity must be taken into account when determining levels of ozone. On the relative humidity–ozone chart (Figure 2), find the Schonbein ozone number of one of the pieces of ozone paper on the scale along the bottom of the chart. Draw a line up from this number, until it meets the humidity curve that corresponds to the humidity at your test location. Read the ozone concentration (in parts per billion) on the left-hand-side of the chart.

5. Repeat step 4, using the Schonbein ozone numbers from each location.

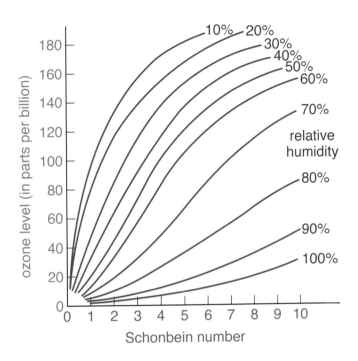

Figure 2

6. Share your findings with those of your classmates. Compare the amount of ozone in different parts of your community.

Analysis

1. Explain the difference in stratospheric and trophospheric ozone.
2. Why is ground-level ozone dangerous?
3. How much ozone did you find in areas that you tested?
4. Were your findings the same as those of your classmates? Explain why or why not.
5. Why do you need to know the relative humidity to calculate ozone levels?

What's Going On?

The German-Swiss scientist Christian Freidrich Schönbein (1799–1868) discovered ozone in 1840. Schönbein developed a test paper to indicate the presence, and relative amount, of ozone. The paper changed color because ozone oxidizes potassium iodide into iodine. The reaction is:

$$2 \, KI + O_3 + H_2O \rightarrow 2KOH + O_2 + 2 \, I$$

The iodine reacts with starch in the paper and gives it a purple color. The exact shade of purple depends on how much ozone is present. The Schönbein color scale can be used to translate color to levels of ozone.

Ozone levels in a community can vary from one location to another as well as by time of day. Although one might expect ozone levels to be highest in areas of heavy traffic, ozone is carried by wind from its source to other locations. For this reason, people living in rural areas may experience as much ozone as those living in cities.

Connections

Ozone is measured in parts per billion (ppb). Air that is not polluted contains 10 to 15 ppb ozone. The Environmental Protection Agency (EPA) has determined that 80 ppb of ozone over a period of 8 hours can be dangerous to one's health. In heavily populated regions, levels may reach 125 ppb when the weather is hot and stagnant.

The EPA has established the Air Quality Index (AQI), a color-coded tool that reflects the quality of air (see the data table on page 61). According to the index, ozone levels above 75 ppb are considered unhealthy for sensitive groups. This level of ozone is factored in with other major air pollutants to reflect air quality labeled as "code orange." Sensitive groups include children, people who have asthma and other lung diseases, and older adults. The four other major air pollutants are particulate matter, carbon monoxide, sulfur dioxide, and nitrogen dioxide. Individuals can reduce their exposure to ozone and other air pollutants by reducing the amount of time they spend outdoors or adjusting the time of day when they are active outdoors. Ozone levels are higher in the afternoons, so mornings are better times for walking or jogging than midday.

 Want to Know More?

See appendix for Our Findings.

Further Reading

California Environmental Protection Agency. "The Physics and Chemistry of Ozone." Available online. URL: http://www.fraqmd.org/OzoneChemistry.

Data Table		
Air quality Index (AQI) values	**Levels of health concern**	**colors**
When the AQI is in this range:	**...air quality conditions are:**	**... as symbolized by this color:**
0 to 50	good	green
51 to100	moderate	yellow
101 to 150	unhealthy for sensitive groups	orange
151 to 200	unhealthy	red
201 to 300	very unhealthy	purple
301 to 500	hazardous	maroon

htm. Accessed June 19, 2008. The formation of ozone and the roles it plays in the atmosphere are explained in easy-to-read language on this Web site.

Environmental Education for Kids. "Good Ozone, Bad Ozone," Wisconsin Department of Natural Resources, June 2008. Available online. URL: http://www.dnr.state.wi.us/Org/caer/ce/eek/earth/air/badozone.htm. Accessed June 19, 2008. This Web page explains the differences in trophospheric and stratospheric ozone.

Rubin, Mordecai B. "The History of Ozone, The Schönbein Period, 1839 to 1868," 2006. Available online. URL: http://www.scs.uiuc.edu/~mainzv/HIST/awards/OPA%20Papers/2001-Rubin.pdf. Accessed June 19, 2008. This is an excellent article on the discovery of, and early work with, ozone.

11. Biodegradation of Oil

Topic

Some bacteria found in the soil have the ability to break down oil.

Introduction

The term *oil spill* brings to mind visions of oil-soaked birds and slick seashores. Oil spills are the accidental releases of large amounts of petroleum. The wreck of the oil tanker the *Exxon Valdez* in Prince William Sound, Alaska, in 1989, released 10.9 million gallons (gal) (41.2 liters [L]) of oil that eventually covered 1,100 miles (1,770 kilometers [km]) of coastline (see Figure 1). Since that time, oil spills have been given much more attention at the national and international levels. Despite legislation to reduce the potential for spills, they can still occur. As the number of off-shore oil wells increases, the likelihood of new spills increases.

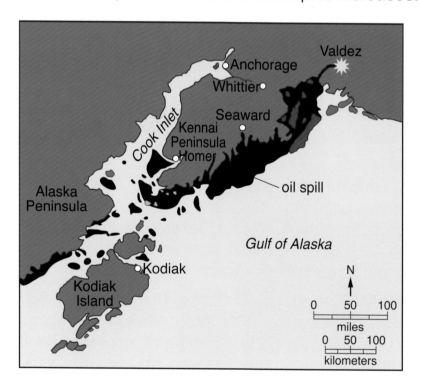

Figure 1

Region of the *Exxon Valdez* oil spill

Scientists are working hard to find ways to contain and clean up future spills. One of the most promising solutions is a simple one: oil-eating bacteria. Some species of *aerobic*, or oxygen-using, bacteria consume oil because it contains carbon, an element that is also found in foods like sugar and starch. Oil-eating bacteria break down carbon compounds to get the energy they need for their metabolic processes. Waste products of oil digestion are carbon dioxide and water (see Figure 2).

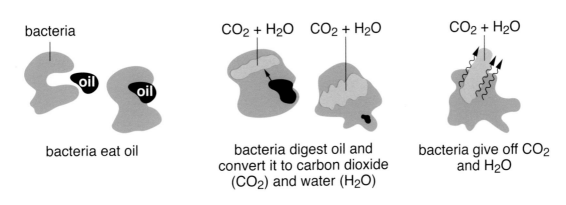

bacteria

bacteria eat oil

$CO_2 + H_2O$ $CO_2 + H_2O$

bacteria digest oil and convert it to carbon dioxide (CO_2) and water (H_2O)

$CO_2 + H_2O$

bacteria give off CO_2 and H_2O

Figure 2

Oil-eating bacteria can naturally be found in soils, especially those where oil is present. In this experiment, you will test soil from three different sources to find out which one contains the most oil-eating microbes.

Time Required

55 minutes on day 1
15 minutes on follow-up days

Materials

- 4 quart jars or 500-milliliter (ml) beakers
- graduated cylinder
- lightweight machine oil (small can)
- 4 aquarium pumps
- aquarium tubing (about 1 foot [ft] [30.5 centimeters(cm)]) for each aquarium pump)
- 4 graduated pipettes

- 4 squares of aluminum foil (large enough to cover jars loosely)
- 0.3 grams (g) of ammonium phosphate
- 0.1 g of magnesium sulfate
- 0.3 g of potassium phosphate
- 1.5 g noniodinated sodium chloride
- 1,200 ml of distilled water
- soil samples from 3 different locations (5 g per sample)
- 20 pieces brown paper, each 4 inches (in.) (10 cm) square
- labels or masking tape
- permanent pen or marker
- ruler
- science notebook

Safety Note   Wear gloves and safety glasses or goggles when working with chemicals and bacteria. Please review and follow the safety guidelines at the beginning of this volume.

Procedure: Day 1

1. Place 300 ml of water and 10 ml of oil in each beaker (or jar).
2. To each beaker, add the following inorganic nutrients: 1.5 g noniodinated sodium chloride, 0.3 g ammonium phosphate, 0.3 g potassium phosphate, 0.1 magnesium sulfate.
3. Label the beakers as A, B, C, and D. Beaker A will serve as the control.
4. Place 5 g of soil from one location in beaker B. Describe the source of this soil sample in the second column of the data table.
5. Repeat step 4 for beakers C and D.
6. Set up the air pumps and tubing so that each beaker contains a tube that bubbles air into the bottom of the container. This will ensure that the mixtures are supplied with air.
7. Estimate the amount of oil in each beaker with an oil spot test. To perform the test:

a. Use the permanent black pen and ruler to divide 4 pieces of brown paper into grids of 16 squares.

b. In the upper left-hand corner, label the papers as "A," "B," "C," and "D."

c. Label the pipettes as "A," "B," "C," and "D."

d. With pipette A, collect 1 ml of water from jar or beaker A. Take the water sample from just below the surface.

e. Place the water in the center of the paper labeled A.

f. Repeat steps D and E for the other 3 jars (beakers).

g. Set the papers aside for a few hours. As the water dries, a spot of oil will be left on the paper.

h. Measure the size of each oil spot according to how many grids it covers. For example, the oil spot shown in Figure 3 covers two complete squares on the grid and one-half of four more squares for a total of six squares.

i. Record the size of the oil spot in the column headed "start" on the data table.

8. Loosely cover the beakers with aluminum foil to prevent evaporation and set the beakers aside for one week.

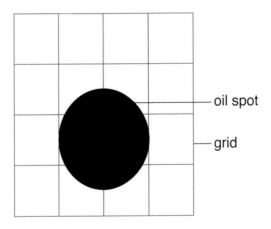

Figure 3

Procedure: Follow-up Days

1. Once a week for 4 weeks, repeat the oil spot test for each jar (beaker). Record the size of the spots on the data table.

Data Table

	Source of soil	Size of oil spot				
		Start	Week 1	Week 2	Week 3	Week 4
A	N/A					
B						
C						
D						

Analysis

1. Explain the oil spot test.
2. Why do some bacteria break down oil?
3. Why do you think the inorganic nutrients were added to each beaker?
4. Which soil sample contained the most oil-eating bacteria? How do you know?
5. Why is it important to have a control in this experiment?
6. Suggest some everyday uses of oil-eating bacteria.

What's Going On?

Bacteria have been on Earth for about 3 billion years, a much longer time than humans, who have existed for a million years. Over that long span of time, bacteria have evolved to live in every niche and corner of the planet. Millions of years ago, some of the bacteria located in oil-saturated soils underwent mutations that produced enzymes capable of breaking down, or digesting, oil. As a result, these bacteria could use oil as a source of food. Oil-digesting bacteria are relatively rare in most soils, but are much more abundant in soils that are contaminated with oil products. Soil from garages, roadways, and old dumping grounds have relatively large populations of oil-eating bacteria.

Scientists have been trying to identify all of the species of bacteria that can break down oil. One species, *Alcanivorax borkumensis*, is a rod-shaped microbe. In unpolluted portions of the ocean, *A. borkumensis* are present, but populations are very small. However, when an oil-spill occurs, these microbes multiply quickly and in a short time dominate the bacterial flora.

Connections

The procedures employed in cleaning oil spills involve several technologies. One simple, but very useful, strategy is spraying the oil spill with dispersants, detergent-like agents that break large volumes of oil into smaller globules. When oil is separated into droplets, bacteria can surround and digest it.

In discussions of oil-eating bacteria, two terms are commonly confused: *biodegradation* and *bioremediation*. Biodegradation is the natural process in which bacteria break down oil into energy and simpler compounds. If oil is spilled on the ground or in the ocean, it will eventually be biodegraded by bacteria in the environment. Bioremediation refers to the products and processes that people employ to speed up biodegradation. One method of bioremediation is to spray an oil spill with cultures of oil-eating bacteria. Bioremediation can also include adding nutrients to bacterial colonies and improving the oxygen supply to bacteria.

Some scientists who work in bioremediation hope to develop bacteria that are super oil-eaters. Through *genetic engineering*, these scientists have developed bacteria that yield unusually high levels of the enzymes needed to digest oil. These bacteria are described as *transgenic organisms* because their DNA has been modified. By applying super oil-eating bacteria to spills, scientists expect to speed the breakdown of oil so that less environmental damage takes place.

 Want to Know More?

See appendix for Our Findings.

Further Reading

Chong, Wu. "Strain of oil-eating bacteria isolated," *China Daily*, March 20, 2007. Available online. URL: http://www.chinadaily.com.cn/china/2007-03/20/content_832106.htm. Accessed June 21, 2008.

Chong explains how a new oil-eating microbe was found and how it might be used to help clean oil spills.

Shah, Archit Sheth. "Marine Biotechnology," 2007. Available online. URL: http://74.125.47.132/search?q=cache:K5vPQPXRDJkJ:cosmos.ucdavis.edu/Archive/2007/FinalProjects/Cluster%25201/Sheth-Shah_Archit_MarineBiotechnology.ppt256,1,Marine%20Biotechnology. Accessed June 24, 2008. Shah describes bacteria that can help break down the oil.

Valdez Convention and Visitors Bureau. "Exxon Valdez Oil Spill," 2007. Available online. URL: http://www.valdezalaska.org/history/oilSpill.html. Accessed June 24, 2008. This Web site provides a review of the events of the *Exxon Valdez* oil spill.

12. The Taste Test

Topic

A survey can help clarify the reasons that people select bottled water over tap water.

Introduction

Bottled water is one of the most popular beverages on the market, and its popularity is on the increase. Why do people select bottled water over tap water? Convenience is definitely one reason. Consumers find it much easier to buy water from a vending machine than to carry a reusable container to and from work or school. The other primary concern is taste. Water's taste is due primarily to three factors: source, mineral content, and treatment. The sources of water include *surface water*, such as lakes and rivers, and *groundwater*, which includes wells, and *aquifers* (see Figure 1). Water's mineral content depends on its source; some areas are naturally higher in calcium and magnesium. These minerals give water a flavor that some people prefer.

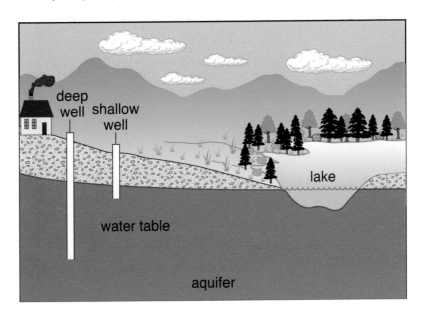

Figure 1

Treatment includes all the processes used to kill microbes and remove contaminants from water. Chlorine is the least expensive and easiest way to kill germs, but it has the disadvantage of leaving an aftertaste. Other methods include treatment with *ozone*, a highly reactive form of oxygen, or ultraviolet (UV) light. Reverse osmosis forces water through a membrane that filters out contaminants (see Figure 2). Distillation is a process in which water is heated to evaporate the pure water, leaving behind its impurities.

Despite all of the variables that can affect water's taste, many contend that individuals cannot really distinguish tap water from bottled water in a taste test. In this experiment, you will conduct a blind taste test find out peoples' preference for water.

Reverse osmosis

tap water

untreated water

membrane

pure water

contaminants

Figure 2

Time Required

55 minutes

Materials

-   2 brands of bottled water
-   tap water
-   6 plastic cups

- ❧ labels
- ❧ waterproof pen or marker
- ❧ science notebook

Safety Note Please review and follow the safety guidelines at the beginning of this volume.

Procedure

1. Using the waterproof pen or pencil, label the bottoms of the three plastic cups as "A," "B," and "C."

2. Pour a little tap water into one of the cups and different brands of bottled water into the other two cups. Make sure that all three water samples are at about the same temperature (about room temperature or chilled in the refrigerator).

3. Ask a volunteer to test all three samples of water for taste. Do not let the volunteer look at the labels on the bottom of the cups. Have him or her rank taste preferences as "1," "2," and "3," where 1 represents their favorite taste and 3 their least favorite taste. Record the responses on the data table.

4. Rearrange the cups and wait a few minutes, then test the volunteer again. Record the responses on the data table.

5. Repeat steps 1 through 4 with nine other volunteers.

6. When the data table is complete, add the numbers in each column to produce totals in the last row of the data table.

Analysis

1. Which of the three types of water did most people prefer?

2. Was the winning sample bottled water or tap water?

3. Based on your experimental results, do you think that people select bottled water over tap water because of the taste?

4. What are some advantages of using bottled water?

5. What are some of the disadvantages of using bottled water?

Data Table

Volunteer's Name	A	B	C
1.			
1.			
2.			
2.			
3.			
3.			
4.			
4.			
5.			
5.			
6.			
6.			
7.			
7.			
8.			
8.			
9.			
9.			
10.			
10.			
Totals			

What's Going On?

In a survey carried out by the National Resource Defense Council (NRDC) over a 4-year period, researchers found that up to 40 percent of bottled waters are repackaged municipal water. With this finding, it is not surprising that many people cannot distinguish tap from bottled water in a taste test. In a taste test conducted by the World Wildlife Fund in 2001, most consumers could not distinguish between bottled and tap water. However, many stated that they believed bottled water to have a better taste and to be a healthier choice.

The bottled water industry is huge, estimated at $15 billion in the United States each year, and is growing about 7 percent per year. Several types of water are offered, including spring, purified, mineral, flavored, and vitamin enriched. It is hard for the consumer to interpret all these labels. Spring water, also called artesian, ground, and well water, comes from an underground source. Spring water is collected at the point where it flows out of the ground. Water that is labeled as "purified" can come from any source, but it has been treated so that it is free of chemicals and microbes. Mineral water contains 250 or more parts per million of dissolved solids, usually calcium and magnesium. Flavored water is prepared by adding either natural or artificial flavors such as strawberry and lime. They may be either sweetened or unsweetened. Vitamin waters are similar, but have vitamins added including vitamins C, A, B3, B6, and B12.

Connections

Consumers expect their drinking water to be healthy and to taste good. The safety of water is the concern of two agencies, the Environmental Protection Agency (EPA) and U.S. Food and Drug Administration (FDA). The EPA regulates municipal (tap) water. The FDA regulates bottled water that is prepared in one state and shipped to another. Water that is bottled and sold in the same state does not have to meet either agency's standards.

Most bottled water comes from ground water sources. These reservoirs experience little variation from day to day, so their taste is fairly consistent. Tap water is usually supplied from surface waters, which are influenced by rain and runoff from surrounding land. In addition, tap water is delivered to consumers through pipes, which can affect the taste.

Most tap water is disinfected with chlorine because the chemical is relatively inexpensive and has the advantage of continuing to disinfect even as water travels through pipes. On the down side, chlorine can leave a taste. A few municipalities have upgraded their water purification systems to ozone or UV light, the two processes preferred by bottled water manufacturers. Neither of these techniques leave a taste in water. Two other tasteless processes are reverse osmosis and distillation.

Want to Know More?

See appendix for Our Findings.

Further Reading

Environmental Protection Agency. "Ground Water and Drinking Water," September 20, 2007. Available online. URL: http://www.epa.gov/ogwdw/faq/faq.html. Accessed June 21, 2008. The EPA explains how tap water and bottled water are prepared.

Natural Resources Defense Council. "Bottled Water: Pure Drink or Pure Hype?" April 29, 1999. Available online. URL: http://www.nrdc.org/water/drinking/nbw.asp. Accessed June 21, 2008. This Web site explains the findings of the NRDC research comparing the safety of bottled and tap water.

Peek, Liz. "Bottled Water Industry at a Tipping Point," *New York Sun*, July 24, 2007. Available online. URL: http://www.nysun.com/business/bottled-water-industry-at-a-tipping-point/59028/. Accessed June 21, 2008. Peek explains how people's opinions about bottled and tap water are beginning to change due to environmental concerns.

13. Solar Water Heater

Topic

A passive solar water heater is an environmentally friendly way to warm water.

Introduction

The Sun's energy is generated by nuclear reactions. This energy travels through space as *electromagnetic radiation*. Earth retains about 51 percent of the solar energy that strikes it. The rest of the energy is reflected back into space, absorbed, or carried back to the upper atmosphere by *conduction*. Figure 1 shows the details of the Earth's energy budget. Solar energy is changed to heat when it strikes objects on Earth. You have probably experienced the conversion of sunlight into heat if you've ever stood in a sunny spot on a cold winter day.

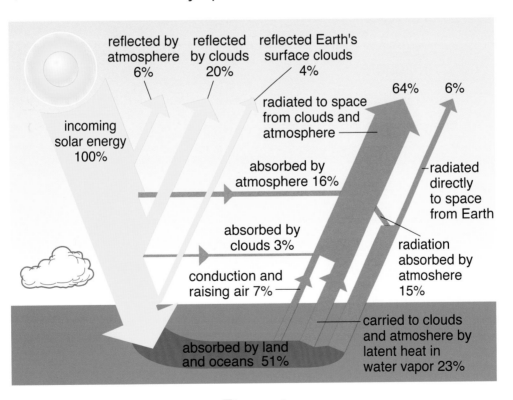

Figure 1

Earth's energy budget

Because solar energy is free and plentiful, it is a logical source of energy to meet the needs of our daily life. There are three basic methods of collecting solar energy: passive solar heating, active solar heating, and photovoltaic cells. Passive solar heating is the simplest; it does not require any mechanical or electrical parts. In this type of system, sunlight strikes and warms air or water. In active solar devices, sunlight is focused on heat collectors using mirrors or lenses. Photovoltaic cells contain materials that release electrons when struck by sunlight. These devices are capable of producing electrical current.

Of the three techniques, passive solar heating of air and water is the oldest and most frequently used. The amount of heat that a passive solar device can collect depends on its design. In this experiment, you will design a passive solar water heater and monitor the temperature of water.

Time Required

55 minutes

Materials

- heavy-gauge black plastic (about 2 feet [ft] [61 centimeters (cm)] square)
- heavy-gauge transparent plastic (about 2 ft [61 cm] square)
- heavy-gauge opaque plastic (about 2ft [61 cm] square)
- 1-gallon Ziploc™ bag (freezer)
- empty 2-liter (L) plastic bottle
- empty 1-L plastic bottle
- plastic tubing (several feet long)
- rubber or cork stoppers
- modeling clay
- soil (about 1 L)
- insulating material (such as fabric)
- scissors
- labels

- glue
- duct tape
- permanent black pen or marker
- thermometers
- science notebook

Safety Note   Please review and follow the safety guidelines at the beginning of this volume.

Procedure

1. Your job is to design and construct a passive solar water heater.
2. You can use any of the supplies provided by your teacher, but you will not need to use all of them.
3. Before you conduct your experiment, decide exactly what you are going to do. Write the steps you plan to take (your experimental procedure) and the materials you plan to use (materials list) on Data Table 1. Show your procedure and materials list to the teacher. If you get teacher approval, proceed with your experiment. If not, modify your work and show it to your teacher again.
4. Once you have teacher approval, assemble the materials you need and begin your procedure.
5. Collect data that indicates how well your design warms water over a 20-minute period. Record your results on Data Table 2.

Analysis

1. Explain the difference between passive and active solar water heaters. What are some advantages of each?
2. Most electric and gas hot water heaters keep water warm once it reaches the desired temperature. Suggest some ways to modify your design to keep water warm.
3. Suggest two improvements you could make to your water heater.
4. Suggest three ways to use water that is heated by solar energy.

5. What are some limitations of a solar water heater?

Data Table 1	
Your experimental procedure	
Your materials list	
Teacher's approval	

Data Table 2	
Time in minutes	**Temperature**
0 (Start)	
5	
10	
15	
20	

What's Going On?

Passive solar water heaters are useful because they make it possible to convert some of the Sun's electromagnetic energy into heat. This heat warms a volume of water, which can be used for anything from bathing to washing dishes. Commercial passive solar hot water heaters fill large containers or tubes with water. These containers are generally made of a black, nonreflective material that absorbs plenty of energy. As the water heats, it can then be routed into a storage tank from which consumers can draw out the water as they need it. Storage tanks are more apt to maintain the heat in the water if they are well insulated.

Water is an ideal choice for a passive solar collector because it has a high *specific heat*. The amount of heat required to raise the temperature of one gram (g) of a material by 1 degree Celsius (°C) is its specific heat. The specific heat of water is 1 calorie/g°C. This is much higher than other liquids. For example, ethyl alcohol has a specific heat of 0.6 calorie/g°C. Because of this characteristic, water's temperature changes slowly as it absorbs or loses heat. In other words, water resists changing temperature. Therefore, once it is heated, it holds on to that heat much longer than other materials.

Connections

A personal solar shower is a simple passive solar water heater. A solar shower is basically a large plastic bag, one side of which is black and the other side transparent. The bottom of the bag is fitted with a hose and a nozzle. The top of the bag has a hanging loop (see Figure 2). During daylight hours, the bag is filled with water and laid on a sunny patch of ground. The water will continue to heat up as long as it is in the Sun. Once the water heats up, it can be used for a shower. Because of water's high specific heat, it will stay warm for a long time even after the Sun goes down.

 ## Want to Know More?

See appendix for Our Findings.

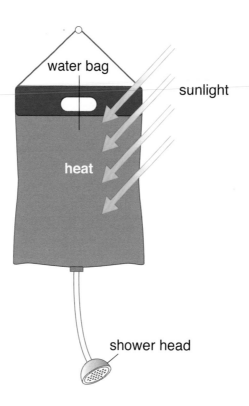

Figure 2

Further Reading

DiscoverSolarEnergy.com. Available online. URL: http://www. discoversolarenergy.com/index.htm. Accessed June 22, 2008. This Web site offers hundreds of links to resources on renewable energy.

Jones, Larry. "Specific Heat," Journey Into Science, March 7, 2007. Available online. URL: http://www.sciencebyjones.com/specific_heat1. htm. Accessed June 22, 2008. Jones explains the chemistry behind water's high specific heat.

North Carolina Solar Center. "Do It Yourself Solar Applications: For Water and Space Heating," June 2000. Available online. URL: http://www.ncsc. ncsu.edu/information_resources/factsheets/23lowcst.pdf . Accessed June 22, 2008. This Web page describes some simple projects for using solar energy in homes

14. Population Growth in Yeast

Topic

Yeast populations with plenty of resources show uncontrolled growth.

Introduction

Yeasts are a large group of one-celled fungi that live in air, soil, and water. Most people are familiar with baker's yeast, *Saccharomyces cereviae*, which is used to make bread. Under the microscope, a yeast cell is relatively large, about 1/100 of a millimeter in width. Like cells of all *eukaryotes*, the outer border of the cell is a membrane that regulates what enters and leaves the cell. Inside the plasma membrane is cytoplasm which contains *organelles* and the nucleus. *DNA (deoxyribonucleic acid)* within the nucleus contains the cell's genetic information and controls its functions. Organelles include ribosomes, which manufacture proteins, lysosomes, which contain digestive enzymes, and endoplasmic reticulum, a system of tubes where several processes occur.

S. cereviae breaks down sugars and converts them into energy to carry out its metabolic processes. Under *aerobic* conditions, when oxygen is present, yeast changes sugar into carbon dioxide, water, and a lot of energy. This process, known as *cellular respiration*, occurs in another organelle, the mitochondria. The equation for cellular respiration is:

$$C_6H_{12}O_6 + 6O_2 \rightarrow 6CO_2 + 6H_2O + energy$$

When oxygen is no longer available, yeasts use an *anaerobic* process called *fermentation,* during which carbon dioxide, ethyl alcohol, and a small amount of energy are produced. Fermentation occurs in the cytoplasm. This chemical reaction is shown in the following equation:

$$C_6H_{12}O_6 \rightarrow 2C_2H_6O + 2CO_2 + energy$$

The carbon dioxide that is produced makes yeast valuable as an ingredient in bread because the bubbles of the gas lift the dough, causing it to rise.

Yeasts multiply by *budding*, a process in which a daughter cell grows on the side of the parent cell. Under optimal conditions, budding takes about 20 minutes. When the daughter cell is complete, a neck forms between the original and the new cell and they separate. In this experiment, you will count the number of yeast cells viewed in pictures of a microscope's field of view over a period of 12 days. The yeast cells were grown in a beaker with sugar and warm water.

Time Required

55 minutes

Materials

- ☞ graph paper
- ☞ science notebook

Safety Note   **Please review and follow the safety guidelines at the beginning of this volume.**

Procedure

1. Examine Figure 1, which shows the number of yeast cells seen in a microscope's field of view over a period of 12 days. Day 1 is the day when a yeast culture was started in a beaker with warm water and sugar. Day 12 is the last day of the experiment.

2. Create a data table in your science notebook in which you can record the number of cells in the field of view over a period of 12 days.

3. Look at Day 1 of Figure 1. Notice that the field of view has been divided into four quadrants. These quadrants were created to make it easier to count cells on a microscope slide. When populations of cells are low, you can easily count every cell on the slide. But when populations are dense, you may find it easier to count the cells in only one quadrant, then multiply the count by four.

4. Count the yeast cells on day 1 of Figure 1 (see pages 83 and 84). Record the number of cells on day 1 in your data table. Keep these things in mind:

a. If one-half or more of a cell falls in the field of view, count it as a cell. If less than half of the cell falls in the field of view, do not count it.

b. If a cell is producing a daughter cell by budding, only count it as one cell.

5. Count the cells for days 2 through 12, recording the counts in the data table.

6. Create a graph that shows the size of this yeast population over a period of 12 days.

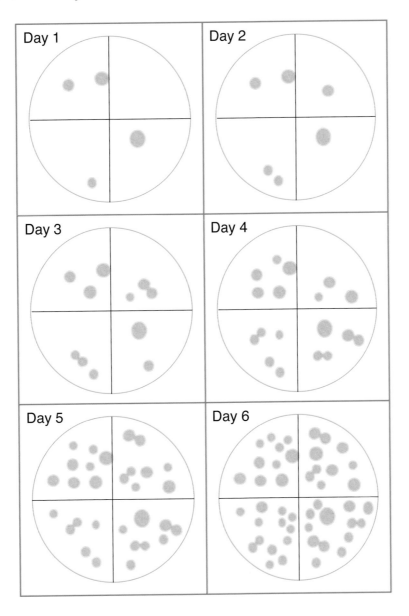

Figure 1

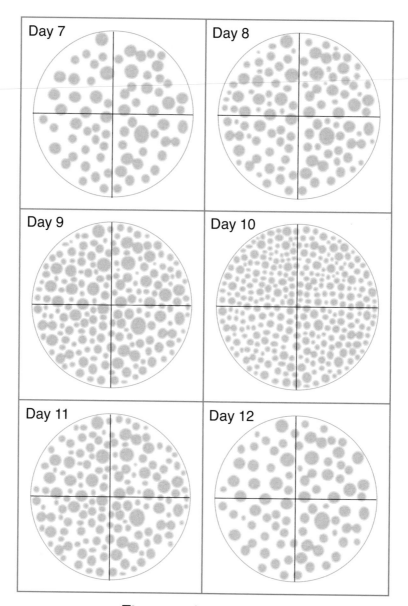

Figure 1 (continued)

Analysis

1. How do yeast cells produce energy under aerobic conditions? Under anaerobic conditions?

2. What substance serves as food for yeast?

3. Why is the field of view divided into four quadrants?

4. When populations grow rapidly, they produce an exponential graph that has a J-shape. Slower growing populations produce a logistic or S-shaped graph (see Figure 2). In logistic growth, populations accelerate until they reach their carrying capacity, then they slow.

Carrying capacity is the maximum number of organisms that an environment can support. Was the growth of the yeast population from days 1 to 10 exponential or logistic?

5.   Based on your graph, on what day do you think that the yeast reached carrying capacity? Explain your answer.

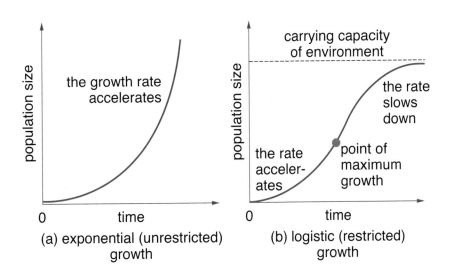

Figure 2

What's Going On?

In this experiment, Figure 1 shows the growth of yeast cells over a period of 12 days. From day 1 to day 10, cells grew rapidly in an exponential pattern, increasing the population size at a constant rate. The graph showed this growth in a typical J-shaped curve. After day 10, all of the yeast's food supply had been used up and the population had exceeded its carrying capacity.

All populations behave very much like the yeast cells in this experiment. When resources are abundant, populations can grow without restraint at an exponential rate. Species that grow exponentially eventually use up all of the resources that are supporting them. When this happens, population size drops dramatically.

Connections

Figure 3 shows the growth of the human population from 8000 B.C.E. through the year 2000. The overall growth pattern of the human population over this period of time produces a J-curve, typical of exponential growth. Since 1950, the human population has increased in size more than it did in the preceding four million years. No one knows when humans will exceed their resources. However, experiences with other populations who grow exponentially have scientists worrying.

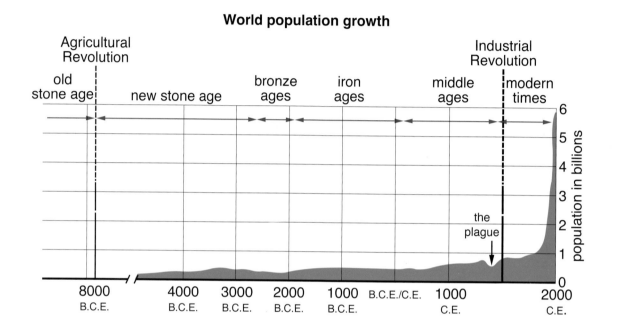

Figure 3

The fast growth of the human population has had a tremendous impact on the environment. The planet's resources are being stretched to the limit as humans expand their domain. Eighty percent of the Earth's original rain forests have been damaged or cleared. Every 20 minutes, one or more species of plants become extinct. More than 40 percent of the groundwater is contaminated by pollution. The United States is one of the biggest offenders in these environmental abuses. Although Americans make up only 5 percent of the world's population, we use more than 25 percent of the resources. One American consumes about 30 times more resources than an average citizen in India. As Americans are using resources, we are causing a lot of pollution. Citizens of the United States contribute 25 percent of the greenhouse gases globally. Awareness of the problems of fast-growing populations is the first step in finding solutions. Everyone needs to be aware of the state of the planet so that we can all contribute to the solution.

Want to Know More?

See appendix for Our Findings.

Further Reading

Global Change. "Population Growth Over Human History," January 4, 2006. University of Michigan. Available online. URL: http://www. globalchange.umich.edu/globalchange2/current/lectures/human_pop/ human_pop.html. Accessed June 22, 2008. This lecture reviews the growth pattern of the human population.

Population Connection. "Population Connection Fact Sheets." Available online. URL: http://www.populationconnection.org/index. php?option=com_content&task=view&id=396&Itemid=18. Accessed June 22, 2008. This Web site provides links to resources discussing the effect of human population growth on the environment.

Volk, Tom, and Anne Galbraith. "This month's fungus is *Saccharomyces cerevisiae*, the bakers' and brewers' yeast," Tom Volk Fungi, 2002. Available online. URL: http://botit.botany.wisc.edu/toms_fungi/dec2002. html. Accessed June 22, 2008. Volk is a professor at the University of Wisconsin who provides information on all types of fungi.

15. How Does Acid Precipitation Affect Coleus?

Topic

Acid rain damages plants in many ways, slowing their growth.

Introduction

As air pollution increases, so do levels of *acid rain*. Acid rain forms when sulfur and nitrogen oxides, gases produced by burning fossil fuels, mix with water in the air then fall to Earth as precipitation. Normal rain, which is slightly acidic, has a pH of 5.6. Precipitation with a pH below 5.6 is considered to be acid rain.

Several metabolic processes in plants are compromised by acid rain, including reproduction. Plants reproduce in two ways, sexually and asexually. Sexually, plants produce eggs and sperm. These cells unite to form ova that develop into new plants. Asexually, plants propagation methods include layering, division, and cuttings. In layering, part of the plant is covered in soil and begins to root while it is still attached to the parent. Later the new plant may separate and become a separate individual. In division, part of the parent plant root is broken off and forms a new plant. A cutting is a leaf or stem that forms it own roots and starts a new plant. The offspring produced in all of these asexual methods are *clones* of the parent. In this experiment, you will design and carry out a procedure to find out how the development of cuttings of coleus (see Figure 1) is affected by various concentrations of acidity.

Time Required

one to two weeks

Materials

- knife
- coleus plant
- plastic cups

- aluminum foil
- pH paper
- vinegar
- baking soda
- straws
- tape
- string or twine
- scissors
- tape measure or ruler
- electronic scale or triple-beam balance
- access to water
- science notebook

Figure 1

Coleus plant

Safety Note   Take care when working with knives. Wear gloves and protective glasses or goggles when working with chemicals. Please review and follow the safety instructions at the beginning of this volume.

Procedure

1. Your job is to design and perform an experiment to find out how different levels of acidity affect the ability of coleus stem cuttings to produce roots. In this experiment, you will need to create several stem cuttings. For each cutting:

   a. Remove a section of coleus stem from the parent plant. To do so, cut the stem just below a *leaf node* using a clean, sharp knife (see Figure 2). A leaf node is place where a leaf grows from a stem.

   b. Remove the lower leaves from the stem and discard.

   c. Place some water in a plastic cup.

   d. Cover the cup with a piece of aluminum foil. Pierce a hole in the aluminum foil.

   e. Insert the coleus stem into the water through the hole in the aluminum foil.

upper leaves

leaf node

lower leaves (to be removed)

Figure 2

2. In your experiment, you can use any of the supplies provided by your teacher, but you will not need to use all of them.

3. Before you conduct your experiment, decide exactly what you are going to do. Keep these facts in mind:

a. A good experiment has a control. Since normal rain has a pH of 5.6, you will need to raise one coleus cutting in a cup of water whose pH is 5.6.

b. You are asked to test more than one concentration of acid on coleus growth. Test the pH of vinegar. If you want to decrease the pH of the vinegar solution, you can either add water or partially neutralize it with a mild base such as a baking soda solution.

c. Coleus stems will produce roots when placed in water. It takes a few days for roots to appear.

d. Healthy coleus stems and leaves maintain their color, shape, and *turgor*, the internal pressure due to water.

4. Write the steps you plan to take (your experimental procedure) and the materials you plan to use (materials list) on the data table. Show your procedure and materials list to the teacher. If you get teacher approval, proceed with your experiment. If not, modify your work and show it to your teacher again.

5. Once you have teacher approval, assemble the materials you need and begin your procedure.

6. Collect your results on a data table of your own design.

Analysis

1. Why does this experiment need a control?

2. What levels of acidity did you use in your experiment?

3. In which cup(s) did coleus stems produce the most roots? Explain why.

4. What does this experiment tell you about the affect of acid rain on plants?

5. Acid rain might damage the plants in an ecosystem without killing them. How might this damage affect the entire ecosystem?

What's Going On?

Both living and nonliving parts of the environment are damaged by acid rain. Plant leaves and roots are injured and growth is slowed. Acid rain can lower or even destroy valuable soil nutrients. Microorganisms that live in soil and help recycle organic matter are also vulnerable to high levels of acidity. Extremely acidic rain may lead to plant death in a relatively short time. Even if a plant is not killed, its growth and development are impaired

Data Table	
Your experimental procedure	
Your materials list	
Teacher's approval	

by the effects of acid rain, making it more likely to suffer disease. A plant whose root system is weakened can lose its grip on the soil and be blown or washed away during severe weather. Acid rain also slows a plant's ability to reproduce. The cumulative effects of acid rain can damage all of the plants in an ecosystem.

Connections

The Clean Air Act of 1970, amended in 1990, was designed to curb the environmental problems caused by air pollution. Environmentalists hoped that the legislation could restrict production of acid rain. Unfortunately, levels of acid rain have not been reduced and new solutions are needed.

Visually inspecting a forest or field may not yield clear evidence of damage from acid rain. Many areas appear to be green and healthy. Closer analysis shows that plants in many ecosystems, especially those in the northeast United States, are severely stressed by the long-term effects of acid rain. Over years, acid build-up in soil has leached nutrients and weakened plants. The damage to soil lasts for years, and will persist for some time even if the problem of acid rain is solved. Leaching causes loss of nutrients. Recovery is slow because nutrients are added to soils by two processes: weathering and decay of dead organic matter. *Weathering,* the erosion of rock into minerals, is a gradual process. Decay of organic matter occurs faster, but still takes decades. Scientists are hoping to find ways to support the plants in damaged ecosystems until they have time to repair themselves. The first step in ecosystem remediation must be a reduction in acid rain.

Want to Know More?

See appendix for Our Findings.

Further Reading

Environmental Protection Agency. "Acid Rain," April 4, 2008. Available online. URL: http://www.epa.gov/acidrain/index.html. Accessed October 4, 2008. This Web site explains the pH scale, the formation of acid rain, and acid rain's affects on living things.

Environment Canada. "Acid Rain," December 19, 2002, The Green Lane. Available online. URL: http://www.ec.gc.ca/acidrain/. Accessed October 4, 2008. This Web site provides comprehensive information on the formation of acid rain, problems due to the precipitation, and solutions.

Smith, Ronald C. "Home Propagation Techniques," North Dakota State University, February, 2004. Available online. URL: http://www.ag.ndsu. edu/pubs/plantsci/landscap/h1257w.htm. Accessed October 4, 2008. Smith explains a number of techniques for propagating plants.

16. Effects of Nitrates on Duckweed Populations

Topic

The size of a duckweed population is affected by levels of nitrates in water.

Introduction

Grassy parks, green lawns, and neatly clipped golf courses owe their vigor and rich color to fertilizers, nutrients that help plants grow. Most fertilizers contain three primary nutrients: nitrogen, phosphorus, and potassium. After a rain, fertilizer that has not been taken up by plants washes into nearby streams, rivers, lakes, and ponds. In these waterways, fertilizer has the same effects on water plants as it did on those terrestrial plants for which it was designed. However, fertilizer levels can accumulate in waterways and cause plant growth to become excessive.

One water plant that responds well to fertilizer is duckweed, or *Lemna minor*, one of the smallest flowering plants. These plants live in still or slow-moving warm water across the globe. A duckweed plant does not look much like a typical plant. It is a single lobe or frond (a leaf-like structure). Fronds often grow in clumps with roots hanging below (see Figure 1). In this experiment, you will raise duckweed in the laboratory and find out how different levels of nitrogen affect its growth.

Time Required

2 weeks

Materials

- 80 duckweed fronds
- 4 petri dishes
- 25 milliliters (ml) of nitrogen solution B

- 25 ml of nitrogen solution C
- 25 ml of nitrogen solution D
- 25 ml of tap water
- inoculating loop
- magnifying glass or stereomicroscope
- permanent marker or pen
- colored pencils
- graph paper
- grow lights or access to a sunny window
- science notebook

lobe or frond

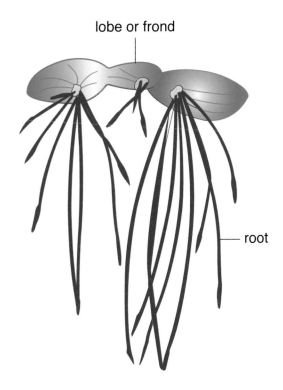

root

Figure 1

Duckweed plants

Safety Note   Please review and follow the safety guidelines at the beginning of this volume.

Procedure

1. Label the four petri dishes as "A," "B," "C," and "D."

2. To dish A, add 25 ml of tap water. This will serve as the control in your experiment.

3. To dish B, add 25 ml of nitrogen solution B, which contains nitrogen at the recommend concentration for lawns and gardens.

4. To dish C, add 25 ml of nitrogen solution C, which contains nitrogen at half the recommended rate for lawns and gardens.

5. To dish D, add 25 ml of nitrogen solution D, which contains nitrogen at twice the recommended rate for lawns and gardens.

6. Use an inoculating loop to transfer 20 lobes or fronds of duckweed to each petri dish. A lobe is one plant, although lobes may be growing in clumps.

7. Place the tops on the petri dishes and set the dishes under grow lights or in a window where they receive plenty of light.

8. Each day for two weeks count the number of duckweed lobes in each dish. Record your counts on the data table. To count lobes:

    a. Use a magnifying glass or a stereomicroscope to view the plants.

    b. Count every visible lobe, even the tiny ones that are just beginning to grow from another lobe. The clump of plants that is made up of four lobes, shown in Figure 2, will give you some idea of how to count plants.

    c. If plant populations are extremely high, draw a four-quadrant grid on a piece of paper and place the grid under the petri dish (see Figure 3). Count the lobes in only one grid, then multiply your count by four.

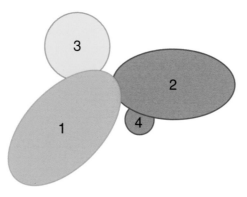

Figure 2

How to count duckweed lobes

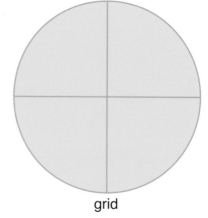

grid

Figure 3

To be placed under petri dish

9. Graph your experimental findings. Place time (number of days) on the X-axis and number of lobes on the Y-axis. Use a different color pencil for each petri dish.

	Data Table			
	Number of Plants in Each Petri Dish			
	A	**B**	**C**	**D**
Day 1	20	20	20	20
Day 2				
Day 3				
Day 4				
Day 5				
Day 6				
Day 7				
Day 8				
Day 9				
Day 10				
Day 11				
Day 12				
Day 13				
Day 14				

Analysis

1. What nutrients are found in most fertilizers?

2. How do fertilizers enter waterways?

3. Describe the structure of one duckweed plant.

4. In this experiment, in which petri dish was duckweed growth the greatest?

5. How do you think that fertilizer runoff into waterways affects duckweed populations? Explain your answer.

6. Suggest some ways to reduce the problem of fertilizer runoff.

What's Going On?

Addition of nitrogen compounds to waterways increases the rate of plant growth. Duckweed is an *invasive species*, one that is not native to the United States and therefore has few natural consumers and diseases. Consequently, duckweed populations grow more aggressively than the native species. When nutrients and sunlight are available and the temperatures are warm, duckweed doubles its mass every two days. The plants quickly spread over the tops of ponds and streams, blocking the light and preventing it from reaching native species below. Such rapid overgrowth of any type of plant or alga in a waterway is known as *eutrophication.*

Even in locales that do not support duckweed, nitrogen in waterways causes problem. Since nitrogen increases the rate of plant growth, it causes water plants to grow rapidly until they form thick mats at the water's surface. When mats become too dense for sunlight and oxygen to penetrate, the plants die and sink to the bottom where they are broken down by oxygen-consuming bacteria. Fast-growing bacterial populations can quickly use up all the available oxygen in the water, depriving other living things of the oxygen they need to survive.

Connections

Natural eutrophication is a gradual process that occurs over decades as waterways age. However, problematic eutrophication occurs because of human activities that create runoff containing nutrients like nitrogen and phosphorus. Some of the primary sources of nutrients in waterways include farmland, sewage treatment plants, and erosion from farmlands and building sites. In a short time, nutrients accumulating in a body of water can destroy the ecosystem within it.

A classic case of eutrophication occurred in Lake Erie in the 1960s, when homes, shopping centers, and expanding farms developed quickly on the land surrounding the lake. With this development came increased runoff, which carried a heavy load of nutrients, especially nitrogen and phosphorus. In a short time, thick layers of water plants and algae developed in the lake then died and sank to the bottom, leading to the depletion of the oxygen in the water. Without this vital gas, animals and plants died. When putrid masses of dead organisms washed onto the shore, communities around the lake decided to make a change. Public concern led to the passage of the 1972 Great Lakes Water Quality Agreement between Canada and the United States. Controls on land use reduced the amount of nutrients reaching the lake, and the lake began to recover. Today, Lake Erie still has problems, but it is in much better condition.

 Want to Know More?

See appendix for Our Findings.

Further Reading

Great Lakes Information Network (GLIN). "Lake Erie," November 1, 2006. Available online. URL: http://www.great-lakes.net/lakes/erie.html. Accessed June 27, 2008. GLIN provides current and historical information on all of the great lakes, including Lake Erie.

Science Daily. "Fertilizer Run-off from Agricultural Activities Blamed for Gulf Dead Zone in Gulf Of Mexico," April 24, 2008. Available online. URL: http://www.sciencedaily.com/releases/2008/04/080421143836.htm. Accessed June 27, 2008. A large oxygen-depleted (or "dead") zone has developed in the Gulf of Mexico due to fertilizer runoff.

Skillicorn, Paul, William Spira, and William Journey. "Duckweed Aquaculture," Agriculture Division, Technical Department of the Europe, Middle East, and North Africa Regional Office of the World Bank. Available online. URL: http://www.p2pays.org/ref/09/08875.htm. Accessed June 27, 2008. In this article, the authors evaluate duckweed as a potential food source for fish raised in aquaculture.

17. Seeds for the Future

Topic

Scientists are always searching for seeds that demonstrate new, useful adaptations.

Introduction

A *seed* is a small, embryonic plant and its food supply, both of which are covered with a protective seed coat (see Figure 1). The food within a seed varies, depending on seed type, but can be starch, oil, or protein. Seeds are *dormant,* or in an inactive state, until conditions for growth are just right. When temperature and light are appropriate, seeds begin to take in oxygen and water, which leads to *germination*, the development of a plant (see Figure 2).

Scientists are actively looking for new seeds that may have undergone natural *mutations,* or changes in DNA, that improve their ability to survive. Any trait that helps an organism survive is an *adaptation*. In this experiment, you will expose seeds to ultraviolet (UV) radiation to see if the resulting plants show any new characteristics.

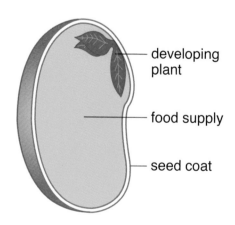

developing plant

food supply

seed coat

Figure 1

Seed

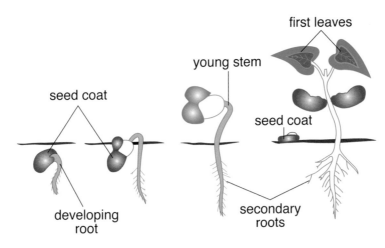

Figure 2

Germination of a bean

Time Required

2 weeks

Materials

- 20 radish seeds
- UV light
- UV light safety goggles
- potting soil
- 2 medium-size pots
- ruler
- permanent pen or marker
- paper towels
- access to water
- grow lights or access to sunny window
- science notebook

Safety Note   Do not look directly into the UV light. Wear UV protective safety goggles when working with a UV light. Please review and follow the safety guidelines at the beginning of this volume.

Procedure: Day 1

1. Place 10 seeds on a paper towel.
2. Wearing UV light goggles, position the seeds about 6 inches (in.) (15.2 centimeters [cm]) under the UV light. Leave the seeds in the UV light overnight.

Procedure: Day 2

1. Label one pot as "UV" and the other as "control."
2. Place soil in each pot.
3. Plant the 10 seeds exposed to UV radiation in the "UV" pot. Place the 10 seeds that were not exposed to UV radiation in the "control" pot. To plant radish seedlings, gently push them into the soil to a depth of about 0.5 in. (1.3 cm).
4. Water each pot with the same amount of water so that the soil in the pots is damp but not soaked.
5. Place the pots in the sunlight or under grow lights.

Procedure: Follow-up Days

1. Each day, check on the condition of the plants in the pots. Notice whether or not the seeds have germinated. As the stems form and the leaves appear, notice the color, shape, size, and condition of the leaves. Record these observations in your science notebook.

Procedure: Final Day

1. Remove the plants from the "UV" pot, brush the soil from the roots, and lay the plants side by side on paper towels.
2. Remove the plants from the "control" pot, brush the soil from the roots, and lay the plants side by side on paper towels.
3. Use the ruler to compare the overall size of the plants and the length of the roots. Record your observations in your science notebook.

Analysis

1. What is a plant adaptation?
2. Why are scientists looking for new seeds?

3. Which group of plants showed more growth, the controls or those exposed to UV radiation? Explain your answer.

4. Which group of plants had the healthier looking leaves, the controls or those exposed to UV radiation? Consider a healthy looking leaf to have deep green color and normal shape. Compare the leaves of your radish seedlings to those in Figure 3.

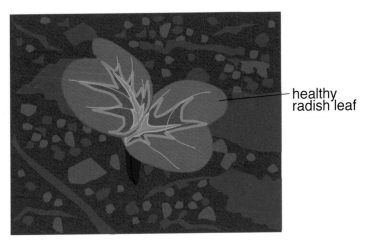

healthy radish leaf

Figure 3

5. Which group of plants had the larger roots, the controls or those exposed to UV radiation? Explain your answer.

6. If you wanted to develop some corn seeds that survive well in areas that are highly polluted with acids, what kind of experiments might you perform?

What's Going On?

Future climatic conditions on Earth may be slightly different than those today. New plant diseases are emerging that may threaten current crops. Insects are constantly evolving, becoming better able to live on existing plants. Because of these constant changes, plants will evolve to be more resistant to disease and insects. The more genetic diversity there is among plants, the better chance they have of producing offspring that can survive.

In nature, plants and seeds are exposed to mutation-causing agents such as chemicals and radiation from space and the Sun. The natural mutation rate is slow, but it does produce some new species. *Mutation breeding* is a technique that speeds up the rate of evolution. A few of the mutated offspring may possess traits that help them resist pests, severe climatic changes, and chemicals in pesticides.

Connections

The concept of mutation breeding began with an experiment by Lewis J. Stadler (1896–1964) in 1928. Working at the University of Missouri, Stadler exposed barley seeds to X-rays and UV radiation to see how the seeds would be affected. The plants that grew from these seeds were very different from their parents. Although the plants did not display any useful traits, the experimental results inspired Stadler to continue his working on exposing seeds to radiation. Eventually, he developed a type of barley that produced greater yields than existing species.

Interest in Stadler's work spread and lead to the successful production of many healthier, disease resistant plants. For example, scientists in California bombarded rice with radiation. As a result, they developed a shorter, sturdier plant that produced more rice than the parent plants. In Ghana, millions of cocoa trees, the source of chocolate, have died from the cocoa swollen shoot virus over the last 50 years. Scientists exposed the buds of cocoa trees to radiation until they found a mutant that is resistant to the virus.

 ## Want to Know More?

See appendix for Our Findings.

Further Reading

Broad, William J. "Useful Mutants, Bred with Radiation," *New York Times*, September 1, 2007. Available online. URL: http://www.nytimes.com/2007/08/28/science/28crop.html?pagewanted=1&_r=1. Accessed July 1, 2008. In this article, Broad describes some of the success stories in mutation breeding.

International Atomic Energy Commission. "Saving the Source of Chocolate; Ghana Targets Killer Virus," March 24, 2006. Available online. URL: http://www.iaea.org/NewsCenter/Features/2006/Ghana/cocoa.html. Accessed June 29, 2008. This article explain how a virus-resistant form of cocoa plant was produced from existing, diseased plants.

Leubner, Gerhart. "Seed Structure and Anatomy," The Seed Biology Place, 2000. Available online. URL: http://www.seedbiology.de/structure.asp#structure1. Accessed July 1, 2008. Leubner offers extensive information on seed structure and function.

18. Design a Reusable Envelope

Topic

Reusable envelopes save energy and reduce pollution.

Introduction

The *waste stream* is made up of all the things we throw away. A large portion of the waste stream, about 35 percent according to the Environmental Protection Agency (EPA), is made up of paper (see Figure 1). Paper and paper products are components of many items we use daily, including food packaging, paper for printers and copiers, toilet tissue, cardboard boxes, and newspaper. In 2006, about 85 million tons of paper products entered the waste stream, three times as much as 1960.

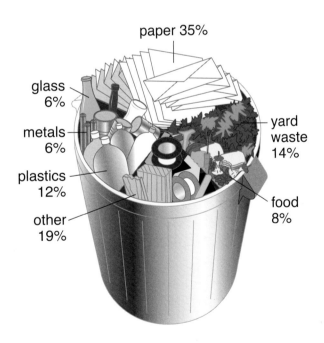

Figure 1

The production of paper requires a lot of energy. Only a few types of industry, notably chemical, petroleum and coal, and metal industries, exceed paper production in energy use. To reduce paper production and save energy, the EPA encourages paper recycling. This technique requires that paper be collected, processed, and added as an ingredient in the production of new paper. Although recycling is a good practice, other energy-conserving approaches are also needed. Creating reusable rather than disposable paper products is one approach. In this experiment, you are going to design an envelope that can be reused.

Time Required

55 minutes

Materials

- copy or construction paper
- glue
- scissors
- tape
- rulers
- transparent fabric (about 2 inches [in.] (5 centimeters [cm] square)
- needle
- thread
- lightweight, waterproof fabric (about 8 in. [20 cm] by 11 in. [28 cm])
- electronic or postal scale
- science notebook

Safety Note   Please review and follow the safety guidelines at the beginning of this volume.

Procedure

1. Work with your lab group to brainstorm a design for a mailing envelope that can be reused at least one time. You can use any of the materials provided by your teacher, but you do not have to use all of them. Keep these things in mind. The finished envelope must be:

   a. able to hold a folded piece of notebook paper.

   b. designed so that a consumer can easily reuse it at least once.

   c. lightweight so that it does not require additional postage. The weight of a first class letter cannot exceed 13 ounces [oz] (368.5 grams [g]), so your envelope should weigh 10 oz (283.5 g) or less.

2. Draw a picture of your envelope design in your science notebook. Show this picture to your teacher for approval before you begin your project.

3. Collect the materials that your group will need to make the envelope.

4. Assemble your envelope.

5. As a group, present your envelope to the class and explain how it works. As you demonstrate your design, your classmates will grade you using the rubric on the data table.

Analysis

1. What are some of the advantages of a reusable envelope?

2. What are some disadvantages of a reusable envelope?

3. Suggest some other ways to reduce the production of paper.

4. Make a list of all the paper products with which you come in contact.

5. Design an ad for a newspaper that promotes the use of reusable envelopes. In your ad, be sure to state all the reasons that reusable envelopes are better for the consumer and the environment than traditional envelopes.

	Data Table			
	Characteristics of the Envelope Assign a numeric grade in each category. Use the scale 3, 2, 1 in which 3 represents an excellent job, 2 represents pretty good work, and 1 represents fair work. Assign a grade of 0 if the work in one category was not done.			
Names of students in each group	Will hold a folded piece of paper	Can be reused at least one time	Weighs less than 10 ounces	Is attractive

What's Going On?

Businesses that send out monthly statements usually include reply envelopes. Each year in the United States, more than 80 billion reply envelopes are included in the mail. Reusable envelopes eliminate the need for separate reply envelopes, reducing the use of paper and saving energy. For every one million reusable envelopes, 250 million *BTU*s of energy are saved. A BTU, or British Thermal Unit, is a measurement of heat energy. One BTU is the amount of energy needed to raise the temperature of one pound of water one degree Fahrenheit. To put this in perspective, more than 71 trillion BTUs of energy are needed to make 80 billion reply envelopes.

The other plus that comes from reusable envelopes is a significant reduction in pollution. All paper products, including reusable envelopes, are made using fossil fuels. In the paper industry, fossil fuels create more than one billion pounds of *greenhouse gases*. Carbon dioxide, water vapor, and methane, the primary greenhouse gases, collect in the atmosphere and trap heat near the Earth. Greenhouse gases have been linked to *global warming*, an overall increase in temperatures worldwide.

Connections

Reusing mailing envelopes is one example of *source reduction*, a way of preventing waste. In source reduction, fewer products are produced in the first place, therefore creating less trash and conserving energy. One form of source reduction is the manufacture of lightweight products. The paper food service industry was one of the first to use this technique when they started making paper plates thinner and lighter weight. To add strength, the new streamlined plates were coated with wax or plastic.

Source reduction can be a personal commitment as well as a business approach. Purchasing items that are designed for reuse instead of disposal is a great way to get started. Instead of using paper cups and plates, use dishes. Avoid buying single-serve food items, which come with a lot of packaging. Use the front and back of every piece of paper. Instead of printing items, work electronically and send messages by email instead of through the postal system. Take cloth bags when you go shopping so that you do not need a paper or plastic bag from the store. The actions of individuals have a cumulative effect that makes a difference in the condition of the Earth.

 ## Want to Know More?

See appendix for Our Findings.

Further Reading

DeRosa, James. "The Green PDF: Reducing Greenhouse Gas Emissions One Ream at a Time," Global Warming Initiatives, May 3, 2007. Available online. URL: http://www.greenpdf.com/graphics/TheGreenPDFRevolution.

pdf. Accessed June 30, 2008. DeRosa explains the impact of the loss of trees and the production of paper on accumulation of greenhouse gases.

Keep Columbus Beautiful. "Source Reduction." Available online. URL: http://refuse.ci.columbus.oh.us/kcb/brochures/Source%20 Reduction%20II.pdf. Accessed June 30, 2008. Columbus, Ohio, has prepared an educational and entertaining brochure to help people reduce the amount of waste they produce.

Story, Louise. "The Hidden Life of Paper and Its Impact on the Environment," *New York Times*, October 26, 2006. Available online. URL: http://www.nytimes.com/2006/10/25/business/media/25adco.html. Accessed June 30, 2008. This article explains how much paper is used in the production of *Time* magazine.

19. Algae As Biofuel

Topic

Some species of algae are good sources of oil that can be used as fuel.

Introduction

The United States runs on oil that is used to make electricity and to power vehicles. Most of the oil in the United States comes from limited reserves deep in the Earth. For decades, scientists have been searching for a renewable, nonpolluting way to provide energy on a large scale.

One result of this work has been the use of plant oil as fuels. Soybeans contain oil that can be pressed from the beans and used to make diesel fuel. Since the fuel comes from a living thing instead of from the ground, it is called *biofuel*. However, there are some problems associated with this technique. Soybeans require a lot of farmland, space on which food crops would generally be grown. In addition, the yield of oil is only moderate, so huge crops would be required to power the nation's cars.

To overcome these drawbacks, scientists have turned to algae, simple, plantlike organisms. Algae offer many advantages over soybeans and other more traditional crops. Algae can be cultivated on land that is not suitable for other crops as well as in *brackish,* or slightly salty, water. In addition, algae yield more oil per pound than soybeans. Recent studies show that algae could produce enough oil to meet all of the transportation needs in the United States on only 0.3 percent of this country's land. Much of the current research has been done with diatoms and green algae, two groups of algae. Figure 1 shows some common diatoms and several types of green algae are in Figure 2. On algal farms, these organisms could be cultured in shallow ponds or tanks. In this experiment, you will test one of the factors that algae grown in cultures require for growth.

 ## Time Required

55 minutes on day 1
30 minutes on each follow up day over a period of two weeks
55 minutes on the final day of the experiment

Figure 1

Diatoms

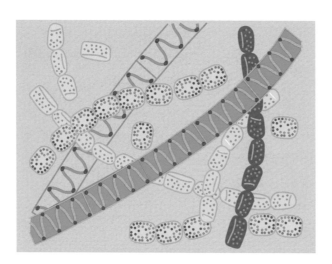

Figure 2

Green algae

Materials

- ➣ 3 large petri dishes with lids
- ➣ graduated cylinder
- ➣ pipettes
- ➣ mixed algal culture (about 20 milliliters [ml])
- ➣ liquid fertilizer (about 20 ml)
- ➣ NaCl (about 10 grams)

- electronic scale or triple-beam balance
- permanent black pen or marker
- black construction paper
- waxed paper
- grow lights or access to a sunny window
- dechlorinated water (about 100 ml)
- science notebook

Safety Note Please review and follow the safety guidelines at the beginning of this volume.

Procedure

1. Your job is to design and perform an experiment to help find the conditions needed for optimal growth of algae. You will grow algae in petri dishes.

2. You can use any of the supplies provided by your teacher, but you will not need to use all of them.

3. Before you conduct your experiment, decide exactly what you are going to do. Write the steps you plan to take (your experimental procedure) and the materials you plan to use (materials list) on the data table. You may test one of the following factors that affect algae's growth: light, temperature, salinity, or availability of nutrients. Keep these points in mind:

   a. A good experiment has a control.

   b. You need some method of measuring algae's growth. In this experiment, use the color of the culture in each petri dish as a measure of growth. As the algae reproduce, the water in which they are growing will become greener and cloudier. Put a piece of white paper under each petri dish to help you judge changes in the algal populations.

   c. Set up your experiment to run for about two weeks.

4. Once your procedure is written, show it to the teacher. If you get teacher approval, assemble your materials and proceed with your experiment. If not, modify your work and show it to your teacher again.

5. Collect your results on a data table of your own design.

6. On the last day of the experiment, finalize your data, draw conclusions, and answer the Analysis questions. Dispose of the algal cultures according to your teacher's instructions.

Analysis

1. Why does the United States need a new source of oil?
2. Define "biofuel."
3. What are some advantages of algae over soybeans as a source of oil?
4. Which algal growth factor did you test in your experiment?
5. What conclusions can you draw from your experiment?
6. Why is the color of an algal culture a good way to measure growth?
7. Suggest a follow-up experiment to the one you just performed.

Data Table	
Your experimental procedure	
Your materials list	
Teacher's approval	

What's Going On?

In this experiment, you raised cultures of mixed algae, an assortment of different kinds of algae. Like plants, algae need light, nutrients, and carbon dioxide to grow. When conditions are ideal, algae can double their population size in two days. Algae require light to carry out *photosynthesis,* a process in which carbon dioxide and water molecules use light energy and chemicals to produce glucose and oxygen. The process of photosynthesis occurs within the pigment *chlorophyll,* which is contained in *chloroplasts.* Algae break down glucose for energy or use it to make other compounds such as complex carbohydrates or oils. Without the right balance of light, carbon dioxide, and nutrients, algae cannot flourish.

Scientists conducting biofuel research favor some species of algae over others. *Botryococcus* is a type of green alga that makes lipids and stores them as globules in the algal colony. Figure 3 shows several colonies of *Botryococcus.* In current experiments, *Botryococcus* and other species are rarely grown in open tanks or ponds. Sunlight only penetrates a few inches, so deep tanks are not useful. Instead, scientists are raising the algae in *photobioreactors,* containers that let researchers control the environment and prevent other species of organisms from invading the environment. Some photobioreactors are long plastic tubes and others are plastic bags (see Figure 4).

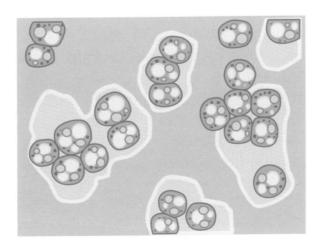

Figure 3

Botryococcus

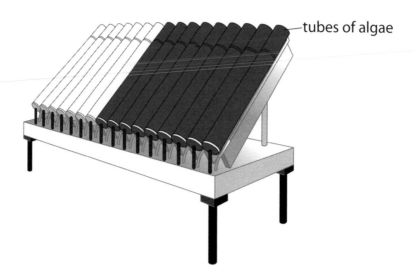

—tubes of algae

Figure 4

Photobioreactor

Connections

Harvesting oil from algae is not the only reason algal cultivation is gaining popularity. Carbohydrates can also be harvested from algae grown in photobioreactors and used to produce *ethanol*, an alcohol that can be burned as fuel. Currently, the United States is focusing on corn as a source of ethanol. Unlike corn, algae require very little space and will not contribute pollutants such as nitrates and pesticides to local waterways. In addition, the protein left over after carbohydrate extraction can be used for animal food. Another exciting factor in growing algae is that scientists are connecting photobioreactors to the smokestacks of power plants, some of the biggest producers of carbon dioxide. Algae use the carbon dioxide in the process of photosynthesis, preventing the gas from entering the atmosphere. Excess carbon dioxide is an air pollutant that is linked to global warming.

Want to Know More?

See appendix for Our Findings.

Further Reading

Metabolomic Fiehn Lab. "Fuel, Biofuel and the Microalgae," March 11, 2008. Available online. URL: http://fiehnlab.ucdavis.edu/staff/kumar/Botryococcus/. Accessed June 30, 2008. On this Web site are several great links to pages on biofuel.

MSNBC Interactive. "Biocrude? Algae-to-oil project aims to deliver," October 27, 2006. Available online. URL: http://www.msnbc.msn.com/id/15250836. Accessed June 30, 2008. This article looks at the advantages of algae over other crops as sources of oil for manufacturing biodiesel fuel.

Roidroid. "MIT Algae Photobioreactor." Available online. URL: http://www.youtube.com/watch?v=EnOSnJJSP5c. Accessed August 15, 2008. In this video, Alan Alda takes a tour of a algae photobioreactor that was located on a roof at MIT (it has since been moved to South Africa), and viewers get a clear and entertaining explanation of the entire process of making biofuel from algae.

Sheehan, John, Terri Dunahay, John Benemann, and Paul Roessler. "A Look Back at the U.S. Department of Energy's Aquatic Species Program—Biodiesel From Algae," U.S. Department of Energy, July 1998. Available online. URL: http://www1.eere.energy.gov/biomass/pdfs/biodiesel_from_algae.pdf. Accessed July 5, 2008. This Web site explains how energy can be extracted from algae.

20. Energy in Ecosystems

Topic

Only 10 percent of the energy from one trophic level is passed on to the next level.

Introduction

Life depends on energy. Most of the living things on Earth get their energy from the Sun. However, only plants and some algae can use the Sun's radiant energy directly. One group of animals, the *primary consumers*, obtain their energy by eating plants. Another type, the *secondary consumers*, feed on plant-eating animals. In a similar way, *tertiary consumers* are those that eat secondary consumers (see Figure 1).

The flow of energy from one *trophic*, or feeding level, to the next is not efficient. Only 10 percent of the energy contained in plants is transferred

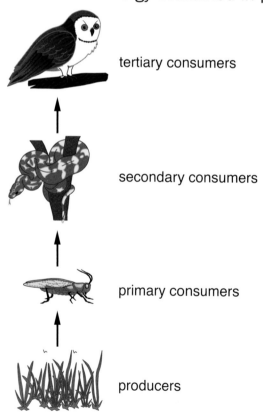

Figure 1

to primary consumers. Secondary consumers get only 10 percent of the energy of the primary consumers. The further the food chain extends, the less energy there is to pass along. This explains why an ecosystem has lots of plants, a fairly large number of primary consumers, a few secondary consumers, and a very small number of tertiary consumers. The movement of energy from one feeding level to the next is represented in an energy pyramid (see Figure 2). In this experiment, you will demonstrate the transfer of energy from one trophic level to another, then draw an energy pyramid representing organisms in a nearby ecosystem.

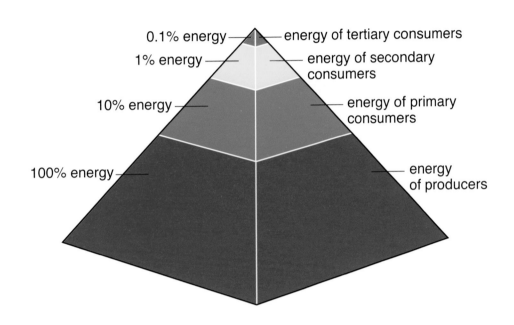

Figure 2

Energy pyramid

Time Required

45 minutes for part A
45 minutes for part B

Materials

- 100-milliliter (ml) graduated cylinder

- 10 ml graduated cylinder

- dropper or pipette
- 1 large paper cup
- 4 small paper cups
- permanent black pens or markers
- access to water
- access to an outdoor area
- science notebook

Safety Note   Please review and follow the safety guidelines at the beginning of this volume.

Procedure: Part A

1. Work with your lab group to brainstorm a demonstration that shows how much energy is passed from one trophic level to another. You can use any of the materials provided by your teacher, but you do not have to use all of them. Keep these things in mind:

   a. In your demonstration, let water represent energy.

   b. One milliliter of water equals 20 drops.

2. Sketch or briefly describe your plans in your science notebook. Show your plans to your teacher for approval before you begin your project.

3. Collect the materials that your group will need to set up the demonstration.

4. Prepare your demonstration.

5. As a group, present your demonstration to the class and explain how it works.

Procedure: Part B

1. With the members of your group, follow your teacher to a designated area outdoors. Sit quietly for about 15 minutes observing organisms in the ecosystem around you.

2. In your science notebook, write the names of all the organisms you see. If you do not know the name of an organism, talk quietly to your lab partners to assign it a "nickname" or number for the duration

of the experiment. For example, if you see three different kinds of butterflies, you could call them "yellow butterfly," "blue butterfly," and "green butterfly," or "butterfly 1," "butterfly 2," and "butterfly 3."

3. Beside the name of each organism in your science notebook, record the number of organisms you see (see the samples in the data table).

4. Label the organisms as producers, primary consumers, or secondary consumers. If you do not know how to classify some organisms, discuss them with the members of your group. If you still need help, check with your teacher.

Sample Data Table		
Kinds of organisms	Number of organisms	Type of organism
Tall tree with flat leaves	2	Producer
Shrub 1	34	Producer
Shrub 2	6	Producer
Grass	241	Producer
Wildflower 1	3	Producer
Wildflower 2	2	Producer
Yellow butterfly	1	Primary consumer
Blue butterfly	2	Primary consumer
Green butterfly	1	Primary consumer
Caterpillars	13	Primary consumer
Spiders	3	Secondary consumer
Blue bird	1	Secondary consumer
Brown bird	2	Primary consumer

Analysis

1. Where do most living things get their energy?

2. Which is the most common group of organisms in an ecosystem; producers, primary consumers, or secondary consumers? Why.

3. What happens to energy as it moves from one trophic level to the next?

4. In your demonstration, what did you use to represent energy? What did you use to represent organisms?

5. Draw an energy pyramid that includes all of the organisms on the sample data table.

6. Draw an energy pyramid that includes all of the organisms you observed outdoors.

What's Going On?

The living and nonliving things in a particular area make up an *ecosystem*. The sizes of ecosystems vary dramatically from hundreds of square miles of desert to a few pints of water in a puddle. A *food chain* represents a series of feeding relationships in the ecosystem. A *food web* (see Figure 3) shows how various food chains in an ecosystem interconnect.

Energy passes through trophic levels of a food chain. Along the way, useful energy is lost as heat at each level. This loss of energy is due to two factors: energy is used by the organisms on each level to maintain life, and the transfer process is not 100 percent efficient. Because the amount of energy available to support life decreases, the numbers and mass of organisms decrease as you move from one trophic level to another.

The number of trophic levels in ecosystems varies. Generally, terrestrial ecosystems have three trophic levels and aquatic ecosystems have four or five. This discrepancy is due to a basic difference in the producers of each system. Terrestrial producers capture the Sun's energy and use it to make glucose and other *carbohydrates*, complex molecules made from glucose. Aquatic producers make glucose and use it to form carbohydrates and *lipids*, molecules that store much more energy than carbohydrates. As a result, the transfer of energy between trophic levels in an aquatic system is more efficient. In addition, the primary producers in aquatic systems are *phytoplankton*, tiny organisms that are completely consumed by very small animals. Every part of a phytoplanktonic organism is used by primary consumers. On land, producers like grasses, shrubs, trees, and other plants have roots, stems, and other parts that cannot be used by primary consumers. As a result, less of the energy captured by producers is passed up the food chain.

Figure 3

Food web

Connections

One of the fundamental organelles in plant cells and some algae is the *chloroplast*, a structure that contains *chlorophyll*. Chlorophyll can capture energy in the process of *photosynthesis*, converting the radiant energy of the Sun into chemical energy in the bonds of glucose molecules. Carbon dioxide in the air is the source of the carbon needed to make glucose. The equation for photosynthesis is:

carbon dioxide + water + Sun's energy → glucose + oxygen

$6CO_2 + 6H_2O + \text{Sun's energy} → C_6H_{12}O_6 + 6O_2$

Animals and decomposers, organisms that cannot carry out photosynthesis, get the energy they need to survive by consuming the glucose made by producers. Glucose is used by all organisms as the primary source of fuel to supply the energy needed for life. In *cellular respiration*, a process that occurs in *mitochondria* of cells, the chemical bonds of glucose molecules are broken and the energy released. The equation for cellular respiration is:

glucose + oxygen → carbon dioxide + water + energy

$C_6H_{12}O_6 + 6O_2 → 6CO_2 + 6H_2O + \text{energy}$

These two chemical reactions, photosynthesis and cellular respiration, are dependent on each other. The products of one form the reactants of the other (see Figure 4).

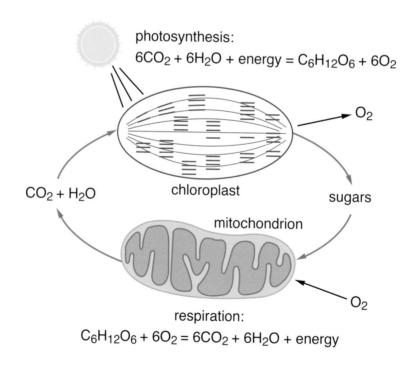

photosynthesis:
$6CO_2 + 6H_2O + \text{energy} = C_6H_{12}O_6 + 6O_2$

O_2

$CO_2 + H_2O$ chloroplast   sugars

mitochondrion

O_2

respiration:
$C_6H_{12}O_6 + 6O_2 = 6CO_2 + 6H_2O + \text{energy}$

Figure 4

Want to Know More?

See appendix for Our Findings.

Further Reading

College of Dupree. "Energy in an Ecosystem," September 25, 2004. Available online. URL: http://www.cod.edu/people/faculty/fancher/Energy.htm. Accessed July 5, 2008. This Web site offers an excellent explanation of the movement of energy through ecosystems.

Pidwirny, Michael, "Introduction to the Ecosystem Concept," PhysicalGeorgraphy.net, 2008. Available online. URL: http://www.physicalgeography.net/fundamentals/9j.html. Accessed February 6, 2009. In this online book, Pidwirny supplies information about the biotic and abiotic aspects of ecosystems.

University of Michigan. "The Concept of the Ecosystem," November 16, 2006. Available online. URL: http://www.globalchange.umich.edu/globalchange1/current/lectures/kling/ecosystem/ecosystem.html. Accessed July 5, 2008. Energy transformations and biogeochemical cycles are discussed in this article on ecosystems.

Scope and Sequence Chart

This chart aligns the experiments in this book with some of the National Science Content Standards. (These experiments do not address every national science standard.) Please refer to your local and state content standards for additional information. As always, adult supervision is recommended and discretion should be used in selecting an experiment appropriate to each age group or to individual students.

Standard	Grades 5–8	Grades 9–12
Physical Science		
Properties and changes of properties in matter		
Chemical reactions		
Motions and forces	7, 9	7, 9
Transfer of energy and interactions of energy and matter	6, 7, 9, 13, 19	6, 7, 9, 13, 19
Conservation of energy and increase in disorder		
Life Science		
Cells and structure and function in living systems	14	14
Reproduction and heredity	17	17
Regulation and behavior	12	12

Populations and ecosystems	2, 3, 5, 8, 14, 20	2, 3, 5, 8, 14, 20
Diversity and adaptations of organisms	2, 3, 4, 8, 11, 17	2, 3, 4, 8, 11, 17
Interdependence of organisms	1, 3, 8, 15	1, 3, 8, 15
Matter, energy, and organization in living systems	1, 7, 11, 14, 16, 18, 19, 20	1, 7, 11, 14, 16, 18, 19, 20
Biological evolution		
Earth Science		
Structure and energy in the Earth system	7, 9, 10, 13	7, 9, 10, 13
Geochemical cycles	2, 4, 5, 6, 7, 11, 15, 16	2, 4, 5, 6, 7, 11, 15, 16
Origin and evolution of the Earth system		
Origin and evolution of the universe		
Earth in the solar system		
Nature of Science		
Science in history	10, 17	10, 17
Science as an endeavor	all	all

Grade Level

Title of Experiment	Grade Level
1. Testing Water for Coliform Bacteria	6–12
2. Effects of Environmental Pollutants on Daphnia	6–12
3. Density of Invasive Species	6–12
4. Do Plants Grow As Well in Gray Water As in Tap Water?	6–12
5. Build and Use a Turbidity Tube	6–12
6. What Do People Throw Away?	6–12
7. Solar Energy	6–12
8. The Safety of Reusing Water Bottles	9–12
9. Wind Energy	9–12
10. Test for Ozone	6–12
11. Biodegradation of Oil	6–12
12. The Taste Test	6–12
13. Solar Water Heater	6–12
14. Population Growth in Yeast	6–12
15. How Does Acid Precipitation Affect Coleus?	6–12
16. Effects of Nitrates on Duckweed Populations	6–12
17. Seeds for the Future	6–12
18. Design a Reusable Envelope	6–12
19. Algae As Biofuel	6–12
20. Energy in Ecosystems	6–12

Setting

The experiments are classified by materials and equipment use as follows:

- Those under SCHOOL LABORATORY involve materials and equipment found only in science laboratories. Those under SCHOOL LABORATORY must be carried out there.

- Those under HOME involve household or everyday materials. Some of these can be done at home, but call for supervision.

- The experiments classified under OUTDOORS may be done at the school or at the home, but call for supervision.

SCHOOL LABORATORY

1. Testing Water for Coliform Bacteria
2. Effects of Environmental Pollutants on Daphnia
7. Solar Energy
8. The Safety of Reusing Water Bottles
9. Wind Energy
10. Test for Ozone
11. Biodegradation of Oil
16. Effects of Nitrates on Duckweed Populations
19. Algae As Biofuel
20. Energy in Ecosystems

HOME

4. Do Plants Grow As Well in Gray Water As in Tap Water?
6. What Do People Throw Away?
12. The Taste Test

13. Solar Water Heater

14. Population Growth in Yeast

15. How Does Acid Precipitation Affect Coleus?

17. Seeds for the Future

18. Design a Reusable Envelope

OUTDOORS

3. Density of Invasive Species

5. Build and Use a Turbidity Tube

Our Findings

1. TESTING WATER FOR COLIFORM BACTERIA

Idea for class discussion: Ask students to explain why water must be purified.

Notes to the teacher: You can add two steps to this experiment by permitting students to test water from a faucet, which should not contain any coliforms, and water from a toilet, which may contain coliforms. In addition, you can permit students to prepare more than one petri dish of their water sample. Prepare a solution of 50 percent bleach for students to pour on their bacterial plates after the experiment.

Analysis

1. 100 ml

2. Answers will vary. The petri dishes were set aside to give bacterial colonies time to develop.

3. Answers will vary depending on water samples tested.

4. The purpose of this test is to determine whether water contains unsafe levels of dangerous bacteria.

5. Answers will vary. Water from the faucet should not contain coliform bacteria.

6. Answers will vary. Water from the toilet will most likely contain coliform bacteria.

2. EFFECTS OF ENVIRONMENTAL POLLUTANTS ON DAPHNIA

Idea for class discussion: Ask students to list some early warning signs of damage in an ecosystem due to pollution. Lead them to understand that by the time we can see ecosystem damage, many populations of the microscopic organisms have been fatally injured.

Notes to the teacher: Solutions (pollutants) to test could include, but are not limited to, salt water, acids, bases, oil, and antifreeze.

Analysis

1. Answers will vary.

2. Answers will vary, depending on students' experiments.

3. Answers will vary, but high concentrations of pollutants most likely caused death of daphnia.

4. The loss of any link in a food chain changes the entire ecosystem. Most daphnia species consume one-cell algae. They provide an important link between photosynthesizers and other small animals.

5. Changes in population sizes of daphnia may indicate that pollutants entering the ecosystems.

3. DENSITY OF INVASIVE SPECIES

Idea for class discussion: Show students samples of two or three plants found in your locale and ask the question: "Where do you think these plants came from?" Lead students to understand that some species are native while others came from other ecosystems.

Notes to the teacher: Designate a large outdoor sampling area that is about 100 square meters. Determine the boundaries of this sampling area so that students can walk along them to find their quadrants for sampling. This experiment has students count species in three quadrants but if time allows, permit them to count five quadrants. After students have calculated their individual group results, pool the class data for a more accurate picture of species density. Before class, determine the invasive species that live in your locale and show students some samples of these plants. Resources that list invasive species can be found in the Further Reading section.

Analysis

1. An invasive species is one that moves into an ecosystem from elsewhere.

2. Answers will vary. Invasive species of plants have no natural enemies, so they spread quickly and use up resources needed by native species.

3. Scientists maintain counts of plant density to see how populations are changing.

4. Answers will vary.

5. Students could count more plots to get more accurate findings.

6. Answers will vary.

4. DO PLANTS GROW AS WELL IN GRAY WATER AS IN TAP WATER?

Idea for class discussion: Ask students to define the term *drought*. Have them suggest some ways to conserve water during a drought. Lead them to understand that some of the water that ordinarily goes into the sewer system could be reused.

Analysis

1. Gray water is water from showers, laundry, and other household sources except toilets and washing dishes.

2. The purpose of this experiment is to find out if plants grow as well in gray water as in tap water.

3. Unless all variables are controlled, the experimenter cannot explain his or her results.

4. Answers will vary. Students might have kept all of their plants in the same general area where they were all exposed to the same temperature.

5. Answers will vary.

5. BUILD AND USE A TURBIDITY TUBE

Idea for class discussion: Show students samples of clear water and muddy water. Ask them to explain the differences in the two samples and the reasons for these differences.

Analysis

1. Turbidity is the degree of cloudiness in water.

2. The disk serves as a marker at the bottom of the tube that the viewer watches as the height of a water column increases.

3. Answers will vary. The tube must be transparent so that light can filter into it.

4. A scientist may monitor several factors that influence the health of the stream

5. Answers will vary, but students will probably get different values. The ability of individuals to perceive the colored disk of plastic through turbid water will vary.

6. WHAT DO PEOPLE THROW AWAY?

Idea for class discussion: Ask students this question: What is the most common material thrown into the trash. After this experiment, revisit the question.

Notes to the teacher: This is a class project, so provide a place (white board, chalk board, overhead project) for students to compile their data.

Analysis

1. Answers will vary by household.

2. Answers will vary by household.

3. Answers will vary by class.

4. Answers will vary by class.

5. 15 pounds; 208 pounds

7. SOLAR ENERGY

Idea for class discussion: Ask students to suggest some renewable sources of energy. Discuss the differences in renewable and nonrenewable resources.

Notes to the teacher: If a sunlit window is not available, use a high-wattage lamp.

Analysis

1. Answers will vary according to experimental data.

2. Answers will vary according to experimental data.

3. The number of rotations dropped when half the cell was covered. This drop was due to loss of half of the energy-producing surface of the solar cell.

4. Answers will vary. Students might suggest using more solar cells or improving the position of the solar cell in the sunlight.

5. Answers will vary but could include street lights, providing energy in remote areas, or solar calculators.

6. Answers will vary, but students might state that solar energy is nonpolluting and readily available.

7. Answers will vary, but students might state that solar cells are expensive and it takes a large number of them to capture enough energy to light a home or power a business.

8. THE SAFETY OF REUSING WATER BOTTLES

Idea for class discussion: Ask students how many of them use water bottles? Find how many students refill the bottles. Pose this question: Could refilling water bottles pose any dangers?

Notes to the teacher: Prepared agar plates should be stored in the refrigerator. Stack them upside down so that condensation does not drop onto the agar. Before use, remove the plates from the refrigerator for a couple of hours so they can come to room temperature. You might want to perform this experiment in conjunction with experiment 12, The Taste Test.

Analysis

1. Answers will vary depending on experimental results, but the petri dish from one of the reused bottles will most likely show the most bacterial growth.

2. Answers will vary depending on experimental results

3. Answers will vary but could include taking swabs on day 1, day 2, and day 3.

4. Answers will vary. Bleach kills the bacteria.

5. Answers will vary. Students might suggest using wide-mouth, reusable bottles that can be thoroughly cleaned.

9. WIND ENERGY

Idea for class discussion: Ask students to describe some problems caused by power plants that rely on the combustion of fossil fuels. Have students suggest some alternatives to fossil fuels. Point out the advantages to these alternatives.

Analysis

1. The voltmeter measures the volts, or electrical potential, produced by the windmill.

2. Answers will vary depending on experimental results.

3. Answers will vary but could include a larger windmill or several windmills working together.

4. Wind-generated electricity does not cause pollution, is inexpensive, and is renewable. Some people do not want windmills in their communities, windmills are noisy, and windmills can be dangerous for birds.

5. Answers will vary but could include using wind to provide power in remote areas where electricity is not available.

10. TEST FOR OZONE

Idea for class discussion: Ask students if they are familiar with the smell of ozone. Explain that they may have smelled it after a lightening storm or when they walk near a copy machine.

Analysis

1. Stratospheric or "good" ozone protects Earth from strong ultraviolet radiation. Tropospheric ozone, or "bad" ozone (in high concentrations) is a pollutant.

2. Ground-level ozone damages delicate tissues in airways.

3. Answers will vary depending on experimental results.

4. Answers will vary. Findings were probably not the same since different individuals perceive color differently.

5. The oxidation of potassium iodide by ozone occurs more quickly and to a greater extent when the relative humidity (which reflects moisture in the air) is high.

11. BIODEGRADATION OF OIL

Idea for class discussion: Ask students to explain why an oil spill is dangerous to ecosystems on shore and in the ocean.

Notes to the teacher: If possible, take soil samples from areas already contaminated by oil. These soils may contain some species that are using the oil for energy. If you do not have access to oily soil, select soil that is rich in organic matter.

Analysis

1. The oil spot test requires that a drop of oil-containing material be placed on brown paper. The oil will give brown paper a translucent appearance.

2. Some bacteria break down oil to use as food.

3. Answers will vary. Living things require both organic and inorganic nutrients.

4. Answers will vary. The soil sample with the most oil-eating bacteria will produce the smallest spot on the oil spot test.

5. A control gives you something to which you can compare your results.

6. Answers will vary. Students might suggest using the bacteria to break down oil in water around docks or to break down oil that washes off of roadways.

12. THE TASTE TEST

Idea for class discussion: Ask how many students think that bottled water tastes better than tap water. Revisit this informal survey after the experiment.

Notes to the teacher: You might want to perform this experiment in conjunction with experiment 8, The Safety of Reusing Water Bottles.

Analysis

1. Answers will vary based on experimental results.

2. Answers will vary based on experimental results.

3. Answers will vary based on experimental results.

4. Answers will vary but could include convenience.

5. Answers will vary but could include the environmental problems created by billions of plastic bottles or the safety of reusing water bottles.

13. SOLAR WATER HEATER

Idea for class discussion: Ask students how many enjoy a hot shower. Have one or two explain how the water in their shower is heated. Briefly discuss the environmental impact of heating water with fossil fuels.

Notes to the teacher: A variety of materials can be made available for this experiment. You can add, remove, or substitute items on the materials list.

Analysis

1. Passive solar water heaters lie in the Sun and collect the sun's energy. They are simple to build and inexpensive, but may not consistently produce plenty of hot water. Active solar water heaters can produce hotter water because they focus the Sun's rays on a collector, then store the warm water to prevent heat loss.

2. Answers will vary. Students might suggest funneling the warm water into an insulated holding tank.

3. Answers will vary.

4. Answers will vary but could include bathing, washing dishes, or heating a room.

5. Answers will vary. If the Sun does not shine for several days, hot water cannot be generated and the system might require a back-up heater.

14. POPULATION GROWTH IN YEAST

Idea for class discussion: Find out how many students like yeast bread. Have students discuss the role of yeast in bread making.

Analysis

1. Yeasts use oxygen to break down glucose, water, and carbon dioxidein the process of cellular respiration. When oxygen is not availalbe, yeasts convert glucose to alcohol and carbon dioxide in the process of fermentation.

2. sugar

3. If there are too many cells to count on the entire slide, one can count the cells in one quadrant and multiply their findings by four.

4. exponential

5. Day 10: the population size stopped increasing.

15. HOW DOES ACID PRECIPITATION AFFECT COLEUS?

Idea for class discussion: Show students a picture of a forest that has been damaged by acid rain. (You can find many such pictures on the Internet. One striking example is found at http://science. nationalgeographic.com/science/enlarge/acidspruce.html) Without disclosing the cause of the damage, ask them to explain what might have happened. Lead them to realize that acid rain damages forests for decades, and the damage is cumulative.

Notes to the teacher: Depending on students' skill levels, you may prefer to offer acids (other than vinegar) for students to use. You could also dilute acid solutions so that students have some with different pHs.

Analysis

1. A control provides a standard against which one can compare their results.

2. Answers will vary.

3. Answers will vary, but best results (best root production) probably occurred in the cup with least acidic levels.

4. Answers will vary. Acid rain reduces the production of healthy roots in plants.

5. Answers will vary. Plants that do not have strong roots or leaves are not able to carry out life processes, which impact other organisms.

16. EFFECTS OF NITRATES ON DUCKWEED POPULATIONS

Idea for class discussion: Discuss the concept of drainage basins with students. Explain how all of the land surrounding a body of water contributes to the runoff into that water. Have students suggest some problems that might originate in a waterway's drainage basin.

Notes to the teacher: Make three solutions of nitrogen fertilizer (ammonium nitrate is preferable) at different strengths. To prepare solutions, rinse out three 1-gallon jugs. Fill each with a gallon of water. Label the jugs "B," "C," and "D." To jug B, add the amount of fertilizer recommended on the box or bag. Mix the fertilizer with the water until completely dissolved. To jug C, add half the amount of fertilizer recommended. Mix the fertilizer with the water until completely dissolved. To jug D, add twice the amount of fertilizer recommended. Mix the fertilizer with the water until completely dissolved.

Analysis

1. nitrogen, phosphorus, and potassium

2. Fertilizers enter waterways through runoff from the drainage basin.

3. One duckweed plant is a single frond or lobe.

4. Answers will vary, but the best growth probably occurred in petri dish D.

5. Answers will vary. Increased levels of fertilizer will increase populations of duckweed.

6. Answers will vary but could include limiting the use of fertilizer near bodies of water and building erosion barriers to prevent materials from being carried to bodies of water.

17. SEEDS FOR THE FUTURE

Idea for class discussion: Ask students where new kinds of seeds come from. Review the concepts of genetic information, DNA, and mutations before the experiment.

Analysis

1. A plant adaptation is any characteristic that helps a plant survive.

2. New seeds may provide traits that are useful such as bigger plants, more protein in seeds used for food, or plants that are resistant to drought or insect damage.

3. Answers will vary depending on students' experimental results.

4. Answers will vary depending on students' experimental results.

5. Answers will vary depending on students' experimental results.

6. Answers will vary. Students might suggest exposing corn seeds to acidic conditions to see which ones survive the best.

18. DESIGN A REUSABLE ENVELOPE

Idea for class discussion: Show students a sample of an envelope that contains a return mail envelope. (You may want to use as an example mail from the Heart Association or the Humane Society rather than a bill.) Ask them to imagine that they are in charge of conserving paper at a business. Ask them what they could do to reduce the amount of paper involved in such mailings.

Analysis

1. A reusable envelope extends the life of a paper product and reduces paper production.

2. Answers will vary, but students might say that a reusable envelope requires special production techniques, that it might not hold up well, or that people might not know how to use them.

3. Answers will vary but could include recycling, writing on the back of paper, and using electronic rather than print copies.

4. Answers will vary but could include notebook paper, cereal box, tissue, paper around snack food, and paper used to print books.

5. Answers will vary.

19. ALGAE AS BIOFUEL

Idea for class discussion: Ask students where we get gasoline. Review the idea that gasoline is a product of crude oil. Find out what students know about crude oil availability.

Analysis

1. The United States is running out of oil, which operates electrical plants, industries, and transportation.

2. Biofuel is oil or other combustible compounds that are made from plants.

3. Algae can be grown in areas not suitable for agriculture and require little care.

4. Answers will vary with experimental design.

5. Answers will vary with experimental results.

6. Deep color suggests that the algae colonies are very thick.

7. Answers will vary, but students might suggesting testing another nutrient factor, amount of oxygen, amount of exposure to light, or set-up of the apparatus.

20. ENERGY IN AN ECOSYSTEM

Idea for class discussion: Students sometimes have the misconception that animals eat only plant leaves, so discuss some of the other plant parts that animals consume. Some examples include acorns, plant roots and bulbs, nectar, and wood.

Analysis

1. the Sun

2. Producers are most common because they capture and use energy directly. The number of consumers depends on how many producers are available as food.

3. Energy is lost as heat as it moves from one trophic level to the next.

4. Water represents energy. Representations of organisms will vary, but students may have used containers such as cups.

5. See the figure below.

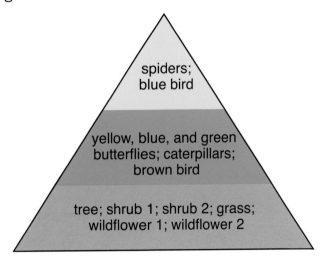

6. Answers will vary depending on experimental results.

Glossary

acid rain   rain that is acidic because of contact with air-borne pollutants such as sulfur oxides, carbon dioxide, and nitrogen oxides.

adaptation   characteristic due to natural selection that helps organisms survive in their environment

aerobic   related to processes that require oxygen

alternating current   electric current that reverses directions many times each second

anaerobic   related to processes that do not require oxygen

aquifer   permeable layer of water-bearing rock, sand, or gravel

biodegradation   bacterial breakdown of complex materials into simpler substances

biodiversity   number and range of species within an ecosystem

biofuel   fuel made from a renewable, organic material such as plant matter

bioremediation   use of bacteria and other microorganisms to break down pollutants

black water   water that contains wastes from humans or other animals

BTU (British Thermal Unit)   amount of energy needed to raise the temperature of 1 pound of water 1 degree Fahrenheit

budding   asexual method of reproduction in which a new organism develops on the body of the parent organism

carbohydrate   macromolecule formed from chains of glucose molecules

carrying capacity   maximum number of individuals that can be supported by an environment

cellular respiration   aerobic process in which glucose is changed to a usable form of energy, called ATP

chlorophyll   green pigment in plant cells that can capture the Sun's energy for use in the process of photosynthesis

chloroplast   organelle in plant cells that contains chlorophyll

clones   cells or individuals that are exactly like the parent

conduction   transfer of heat through a substance by particle to particle contact

cullet   pieces of broken glass prepared for recycling

daphnia   small freshwater crustacean also known as a water flea

density   the mass of an object per unit volume

direct current   electrical current that flows in one direction only

dissecting microscope   microscope used to enlarge and view macroscopic organisms such as small crustaceans and insects

DNA (deoxyribonucleic acid)   genetic material found within a cell

dormant   temporarily inactive as during the period when a plant delays growth

electromagnetic radiation   energy that travels in a wave and has both magnetic and electrical characteristics

enzyme chemical in living things that speeds up or slows down reactions

ethanol alcohol produced by yeast or from the fermentation of corn that can be used for fuel

eukaryotes complex cells that have nuclei and membrane-bound organelles

eutrophication process in which a body of water becomes enriched with nutrients, causing excessive growth of algae

evapotranspiration loss of water from plants through evaporation and from leaves by transpiration

fecal coliform bacteria microscopic organisms found in the wastes of humans and other warm-blooded animals

fermentation anaerobic process in which cells convert sugar into energy, alcohol, and carbon dioxide

food chain feeding relationships in an ecosystem that show how energy is transferred from producers to consumers

food web all of the overlapping food chains in an ecosystem

generator machine that produces electricity when a magnet is rotated in a coil of wire

genetic engineering the insertion, deletion, or rearrangement of genes in an organism's DNA

germination the process in which a seed's embryo emerges from a seed

global warming an overall increase in Earth's temperature caused by the accumulation of gases in the atmosphere

gram staining a staining technique used to differentiate types of bacteria

gray water wastewater from showers, washing machines, and dishwashers that can be used for watering plants

greenhouse gases atmospheric gases, primarily water vapor, methane, carbon dioxide, and ozone, that trap the Sun's heat near Earth's surface

groundwater water that is located underground in the porous part of Earth's crust

invasive species any species that is introduced to an area and is likely to out compete native organisms

kinetic energy the energy of a body due to its motion

lactose the disaccharide sugar found in milk

leaf node the place on a stem from which a leaf grows

lipid macromolecule made of fatty acids and glycerol that provides insulation, protection for organs, and long-term energy

mitochondria organelle that converts glucose into a usable form of energy

mutation change in the sequence of bases in a cell's DNA

mutation breeding process in which a cell's DNA is changed to create desirable genes and new traits

nonrenewable resources natural resources such as oil and coal that cannot be replenished

organelle membrane-bound structure within a cell that has a specialized function

ozone highly reactive molecule of oxygen made of three oxygen atoms

pathogen organism or agent that can cause disease

photobioreactor device that houses algae and provides light, heat, and nutrients for optimal algal growth

photosynthesis   biochemical process in which chlorophyll traps the Sun's energy and uses it to make glucose

phytoplankton   free-floating, small algae that can be found on the surface of fresh water and in marine environments

primary consumers   organisms that feed on plants or plant parts

renewable resources   natural resources, such as wind and sunlight, that are replenished by natural processes

riparian   related to the area next to a body of water

secondary consumers   organisms that feed on primary consumers

seed   embryonic plant and its food enclosed in a protective coat

sewage   solid and liquid wastes from homes, businesses, and industries that is suspended in water

silt   fine soil particles that are smaller than sand but larger than clay

solar cell   device that changes the Sun's energy into electrical energy

source reduction   reduction in the amount or toxicity of waste

stratosphere   second layer of Earth's atmosphere located 8 to 12 miles (14 to 22 kilometers) above the surface

surface water   water in lakes, rivers, streams, bays, and oceans that is located on the Earth's surface

tertiary consumers   organisms that feed on secondary consumers

transformer   device that either increases or decreases voltage

transgenic organism   organism whose DNA has been altered by the insertion of one or more genes

trophic   related to the feeding levels of a food chain

troposphere   lowest part of the atmosphere that extends 5 to 9 miles (8 to 15 kilometers) above Earth's surface

variable   the part of an experiment that is changed

volt   unit of electrical potential or pressure

waste stream   all of the solid wastes produced by a community

weathering   physical and chemical breakdown of rock into soil

Internet Resources

The World Wide Web is an invaluable source of information for students, teachers, and parents. The following list is intended to help you get started exploring educational sites that relate to the book. It is just a sample of the Web material that is available to you. All of these sites were accessible as of March 2009.

Educational Resources

Air Now. "Local Forecasts and Conditions." Available online. URL: http://cfpub. epa.gov/airnow/index.cfm?action=airnow.local. Accessed July 5, 2008. On this government-backed program, you can select a state and access the recent air pollution information.

American Chemical Society (ACS). Periodic Table of the Elements. Available online. URL: http://acswebcontent.acs.org/games/pt.html. Accessed March 5, 2009. This interactive Web page is devoted to the Periodic Table and offers up-to-date information on its elements and electron configuration.

American Rivers. Thriving by Nature, 2007. Available online. URL: http://www. americanrivers.org/site/PageServer. Accessed August 16, 2008. American Rivers presents general information on rivers as well as specific data about rivers in danger.

Defenders of Wildlife, 2008. Available online. URL: http://www.defenders.org/index. php. Accessed August 16, 2008. Defenders of Wildlife works to maintain native plants and animals in their environments. Its Web site provides information on many species as well as on conservation.

Energy Kids Page. "History of Garbage," September 2006. Energy Information Administration. Available online. URL: http://www.eia.doe.gov/kids/energyfacts/ saving/recycling/solidwaste/primer.html. Accessed July 5, 2008. This Web site provides an interesting history of garbage and the problems associated with it.

Energy Star. Available online. URL: http://www.energystar.gov/. Accessed August 16, 2008. Energy Star is a partnership between the U.S. Department of Energy, the U.S. Environmental Protection Agency, manufacturers, and utilities. The group promotes energy efficiency and offers suggestions for conserving energy and reducing the carbon footprints of households.

ENN. "Environmental News Network," 2007. Available online. URL: http://www.enn.com/. Accessed July 5, 2008. This well-organized news site offers a wide variety of the latest stories on important environmental issues, including pollution, climate, energy, and ecosystems.

Environmental Protection Agency. Available online. URL: http://www.epa.gov/. Accessed July 3, 2008. This Web site has links to all topics relating to the environment including acid rain, oil spills, ozone, and recycling.

Environmental Science Group. "Our Environment, The Science Around Us," January 5, 2005. Available online. URL: http://www.geocities.com/rainforest/8393/. Accessed August 16, 2008. This Web site offers easy-to-read lessons on a variety of topics including rainforests and El Nino.

Fact Monster. "Oil Spills and Disasters," 2007. Available online. URL: http://www.factmonster.com/ipka/A0001451.html. Accessed July 5, 2008. This Web site provides a timeline of oil spills from the 1967 accident on the *Torrey Canyon* in England to the 2007 South Korean spill.

How Stuff Works. "How Ozone Pollution Works," 2008. Available online. URL: http://www.howstuffworks.com/ozone-pollution.htm. Accessed August 16, 2008. The production of ozone and problems caused by this chemical are explained in this article.

Krantz, David, and Brad Kifferstein. "Water Pollution and Society." Available online. URL: http://www.umich.edu/~gs265/society/waterpollution.htm. The authors use interesting graphics and clear language to describe some of the basics of water pollution.

MSNBC. U.S. News, Environment, 2008. Available online. URL: http://www.msnbc.msn.com/id/3032493/. Accessed August 16, 2008. This Web site carries current information on environmental issues ranging widely from problems with windmills to the use of seals to study Antarctic water.

National Audubon Society. "Audubon," 2008. Available online. URL: http://www.audubon.org/. Accessed August 16, 2008. The National Audubon Society works to conserve natural ecosystems.

National Geographic. Green Guide, 2008. Available online. URL: http://www.thegreenguide.com/. Accessed August 16, 2008. On this Web site, you can test your "Eco IQ" and learn how to live a "greener" lifestyle.

National Public Radio, Environment, 2008. Available online. URL: http://www.npr.org/templates/story/story.php?storyId=93619388. Accessed August 16, 2008. NPR offers broadcasts on topics related to the environment.

National Resources Defense Council. "Issues, Global Warming," February 9, 2007. Available online. URL: http://www.nrdc.org/globalWarming/f101.asp. Accessed July 5, 2008. This Web site answers some basic questions on global warming, its cause, and subsequent effects.

National Wildlife Federation, 2008. Available online. URL: http://www.nwf.org/. Accessed August 16, 2008. The mission of the National Wildlife Federation is to protect wildlife.

New York Times. "Global Warming," July 5, 2008. Available online. URL: http://topics.nytimes.com/top/news/science/topics/globalwarming/index.html?inline=nyt-classifier#. Accessed July 5, 2008. This Web page provides two short articles on global warming and links to pages addressing many of the issues related to this topic.

The Ozone Hole. "Arctic, Antarctic: Poles Apart in Climate Response," May 2, 2008. Available online. URL: http://www.theozonehole.com/arcticresponse.htm. Accessed July 5, 2008. This article explains how the two poles are responding differently to global warming.

Pickett, Sharon. "Acid Rain Revisited." The Hubbard Research Foundation. Accessed July 5, 2008. Available online. URL: http://www.hubbardbrookfoundation.org/filemanager/filedownload/phpoYit2t/Acid_Rain_Revisited.pdf. This 24-page document clearly explains current problems related to air pollution and the effects of acid deposition.

Science Daily. "Environmental Science News," 2008/ Available online. URL: http://www.sciencedaily.com/news/earth_climate/environmental_science/. Accessed August 16, 2008. Science Daily is an online magazine that supplies articles and links on all topics related to the environment.

U.S. Departments of Energy. Energy Efficiency, and Renewable Energy, August 15, 2008. Available online. URL: http://www.eere.energy.gov/. Accessed August 16, 2008. This Web site provides information on methods and technologies that conserve energy.

U.S. Environmental Protection Agency. Climate Change, July 28, 2008. Available online. URL: http://www.epa.gov/climatechange/index.html. Accessed August 16, 2008. This Web site includes information on past weather patterns as well as global warming and greenhouse gases.

Venkataraman, Bina. "Ocean 'Dead Zones' on the Rise," *New York Times*, August 14, 2008. Available online. URL: http://www.nytimes.com/2008/08/15/science/earth/15oceans.html?ref=science. Accessed August 16, 2008. The author explains how and why expanding dead zones are found in many coastal areas.

Worldwatch Institute. "10 Ways to Go Green and Save," 2008. Available online. URL: http://www.worldwatch.org/node/3915?gclid=CKmDzOvmk5UCFQcVswodDSvsgQ. Accessed August 16, 2008. Worldwatch Institute is a research organization that is concerned with global environmental issues.

Periodic Table of Elements

Key:
- atomic number: 1
- symbol: H
- atomic weight: 1.008

Numbers in parentheses are the atomic mass numbers of radioactive isotopes.

1	2	3	4	5	6	7	8	9	10	11	12	13	14	15	16	17	18
1 H 1.008																	2 He 4.003
3 Li 6.941	4 Be 9.012											5 B 10.81	6 C 12.01	7 N 14.01	8 O 16.00	9 F 19.00	10 Ne 20.18
11 Na 22.99	12 Mg 24.31											13 Al 26.98	14 Si 28.09	15 P 30.97	16 S 32.07	17 Cl 35.45	18 Ar 39.95
19 K 39.10	20 Ca 40.08	21 Sc 44.96	22 Ti 47.88	23 V 50.94	24 Cr 52.00	25 Mn 54.94	26 Fe 55.85	27 Co 58.93	28 Ni 58.69	29 Cu 63.55	30 Zn 65.39	31 Ga 69.72	32 Ge 72.59	33 As 74.92	34 Se 78.96	35 Br 79.90	36 Kr 83.80
37 Rb 85.47	38 Sr 87.62	39 Y 88.91	40 Zr 91.22	41 Nb 92.91	42 Mo 95.94	43 Tc (98)	44 Ru 101.1	45 Rh 102.9	46 Pd 106.4	47 Ag 107.9	48 Cd 112.4	49 In 114.8	50 Sn 118.7	51 Sb 121.8	52 Te 127.6	53 I 126.9	54 Xe 131.3
55 Cs 132.9	56 Ba 137.3	57-71*	72 Hf 178.5	73 Ta 180.9	74 W 183.9	75 Re 186.2	76 Os 190.2	77 Ir 192.2	78 Pt 195.1	79 Au 197.0	80 Hg 200.6	81 Tl 204.4	82 Pb 207.2	83 Bi 209.0	84 Po (210)	85 At (210)	86 Rn (222)
87 Fr (223)	88 Ra (226)	89-103‡	104 Rf (261)	105 Db (262)	106 Sg (263)	107 Bh (262)	108 Hs (265)	109 Mt (266)	110 Ds (271)	111 Rg (272)	112 Uub (285)		114 Uuq (289)		116 Uuh (293)		118 Uuo (294)

*lanthanide series

57 La 138.9	58 Ce 140.1	59 Pr 140.9	60 Nd 144.2	61 Pm (145)	62 Sm 150.4	63 Eu 152.0	64 Gd 157.3	65 Tb 158.9	66 Dy 162.5	67 Ho 164.9	68 Er 167.3	69 Tm 168.9	70 Yb 173.0	71 Lu 175.0

‡actinide series

89 Ac (227)	90 Th 232.0	91 Pa 231.0	92 U 238.0	93 Np (237)	94 Pu (244)	95 Am (243)	96 Cm (247)	97 Bk (247)	98 Cf (251)	99 Es (252)	100 Fm (257)	101 Md (258)	102 No (259)	103 Lr (260)

Index

244II